Elevate Your Enterprise

The Tech Founder's Guide
to Building an 8-Figure
Technology Services Business

Marco Formaggio

Sweat2Scale

www.sweat2scale.com

ISBN: 978-0-6458459-0-7 (paperback)
ISBN: 978-0-6458459-1-4 (e-book)

Ordering Information:
Special discounts are available on quantity purchases by corporations, associations, and others. For details, contact www.sweat2scale.com.

CONTENTS

FOREWORD

Written by Tony Hughes
CEO, Sales IQ Global; best-selling author and speaker

Having more than 35 years of corporate and sales leadership experience myself, I know how valuable it is for business owners to learn from others who have had success in the field. I've helped multiple companies scale to win $100 million revenue clients through my own coaching and consulting. Therefore, it is an honor and a pleasure to recommend Marco's book, *Elevate Your Enterprise*, as an impactful guide to scaling and growing a tech services business.

I've known Marco Formaggio personally and professionally in the technology sector for more than a decade. His exceptional knowledge and expertise are matched by his integrity and character in delivering for his customers and staff. His journey from a mechanical engineer to a successful entrepreneur and business advisor is a testament to his talent and passion for technology services.

Marco's wisdom comes from over 25 years in the trenches with clients and partners, designing and implementing complex solutions that transform businesses. His wealth of practical experience gives him a unique and valuable perspective on growing and scaling technology services companies. His ideas work.

What sets Marco apart is his focus on not just growing a business but also on maintaining a high quality of life. He knows that the journey of scaling a business can be challenging, but he also knows the immense satisfaction and rewards that come from reaching the other side.

With his extensive experience in the field—and his success in founding his own company, Bluleader, a leading SAP customer experience partner—Marco brings real-world insights to this book. In these pages, he guides tech services firm owners through the process of profitable growth, from understanding why having the right mindset is so important to learning the strategies required to reach the peak.

The book takes readers on a journey, starting with the basics of why growth is necessary, going on to dispel common myths, and showcasing the benefits of owning a fast-growing tech services firm. It then delves into how to achieve the right mindset for growth and the importance of niche specialization. The book concludes with a focus on execution, providing a road map for growth using the A3 Strategy and multidimensional accountability.

Marco's passion for driving growth in technology services while maintaining high-quality outcomes for customers is evident in every chapter. I have no doubt that this book will be an invaluable resource for entrepreneurs, business owners, and executives who are looking to grow their businesses and reach their full potentials. I am confident that readers will find this book to be an inspiring and actionable guide to growth and success.

So, if you're looking to take your business to the next level, you will be excited to read Elevate your Enterprise. In the pages that follow, you will benefit from the wisdom—earned and validated over decades—of an inspirational coach, mentor, and leader.

INTRODUCTION

Take a moment to imagine a business owner who has had success in his field for most of his career. This business owner has grown clientele to a point at which he has been able to hire employees and invest in technology, marketing, and sales. Everything was going well for a while, but as time went on, things started to change ... and not in a good way.

This business owner is on every client call, works past 6 p.m. every evening, and alienates his family on weekends in favor of growing the business. He hasn't taken a vacation in five years. He looks tired and out of shape. His stress levels are high, and he is losing sleep at the thought of tomorrow's problems.

Life has become incredibly hard for him, and he doesn't know where to turn. He wants advice, but no "advisor" he's approached has given him a framework for getting off the metaphorical tread-mill. However, he still thinks he's doing all the right things. He convinces himself that he just has to persevere and keep grinding, because "that's how successful start-ups operate."

This individual wants to do good things in his business: to properly compensate his employees, to take a portion of his profits and do something philanthropic, and to be able to enjoy a vacation with his family again. Yet if he took a week away from his business, he knows the whole thing would fall apart.

The fact of the matter is, if you work long hours and weekends and don't take time off, you will eventually run yourself down to 60 percent output or lower. This, too, comes at a cost. Your employees, your clients, your family … they all need you at 100 percent.

We hear a lot about burnout, and this entrepreneur is certainly feeling it. Even worse, a line in the sand has been drawn, and two enjoyable elements of an entrepreneur's life have become an either-or choice: family or business. That choice is fallacious. It's a lie, and it doesn't have to be that way.

This is just one of many scenarios in which individuals seeking help with their businesses may have picked up this book. I wrote this book for them—for you. It was inspired by my own story.

Having been through the business journey myself, it was cathartic to release my thoughts and learnings, to get them out of my head and down onto paper. I realized through this process how much I had learned and put into practice over the years and how valuable this information would have been when I first started out. So, you could say, I am writing this book for my younger self. What factors characterized me back then?

- **A hunger to grow a business.** I had a burning desire to run my own technology services business. This was not just about money or financial reward but also a strong desire to forge my own way.

- **A strong practitioner.** I was a practitioner in my business offerings and had to learn to let these skills go in order to focus on business growth.

- **Lacking relevant advice.** I had many advisors and inputs but not many who understood the industry or who had actually done this before.

- **Frantically spinning the hamster wheel.** I was working long hours and constantly thinking about the business even when not working.

- **Losing sight of the end goal.** I felt ownership over my company but didn't fully see or realize how high the growth potential truly was.

- **Stuck under the ceiling.** In the case of Bluleader, we maxed out at a certain size—$4 million in revenue—and, for a period of time, couldn't break through that ceiling.

If you see yourself in some or all of these characteristics, then this book is for you, and I am happy to serve you.

So, what does the scenario look like when the aforementioned business owner realizes true success?

Well, I believe it's better to go through this journey with me in this very moment (the second-best time to plant a tree is now, right?) than to get to the point of complete burnout and say, "You know what? I'm just going to stop running my business so that

I can live a normal life." The misconception in that statement is that you cannot have both. I'm here to tell you that you can, and you will if you read this book, structure things correctly, and get your priorities straight.

You'll come out a better person if you choose the first option. The journey will not be easy, but the fruits of your labor will be delicious! You'll come out not just wealthier but a better person. Applying these steps to your business will build your character and leave a legacy for your children. They'll look at you one day and see how you went through hardship and turned it around, and that will inspire them to grow as well, because they'll be proud of what Mom and/or Dad accomplished.

As a bonus, you'll be able to switch off your phone at 6 p.m., disconnect from your business on the weekends, book a long-overdue vacation, and eventually vacations (yes, plural). Are you ready to change your business and your life? Then dive in and make the transformation from sweat to scale!

CHAPTER 1

How I Went from Sweat to Scale (and to Sale!)

To properly convey my message and coach you to success, it's important for you to know that at the beginning, I was just like you.

My business didn't start as a multimillion-dollar operation. No, quite the contrary. I experienced many of my own struggles along the way. It was from the ashes of those struggles that I rose and triumphed, having achieved a sustainable level of growth, a scalable business model, and eventually the sale of my business, which has led me to my latest project: making the same thing happen for you.

Along the way, the main question in my mind was always "How

can I get a group of smart people (each a rebel in their own way) to work together and pull in the same direction?" If you can figure that out, the world is your oyster.

How It All Began

I started my business, Bluleader, while working as an SAP architect who was well regarded by my peers. I believed I could do it better than my employers by crafting a more niche-focused business, treating my staff better, and achieving higher outcomes for my customers. All I had to do was start and surely I'd succeed. Easier said than done.

I partnered up with a "business expert" whose recommendation was that to run a successful technical services business, my fellow shareholders should be people who could fulfill different parts of a technical project team, such as a project manager, a technical architect, and a process specialist. There was no mention of business skills at all! So, we proceeded to recruit partners who would be shareholders in the company and who had expertise in each of these areas.

After five years, though, I recognized that this strategy had really set me back. I realized I did not need technical practitioners as fellow shareholders and directors. If you are going to have business partners, they need to be business minded (not great technologists), which seems obvious to me now! What I learned was the concept of having the "right seats with the right people in them," or as Jim Collins says, "the right people on the bus."[1] We made some changes, and once we'd finally got it right, after those five years, the business really started to accelerate.

But back at the start, with the core team established, we proceeded to concentrate on generating consulting revenue. The business was profitable within six months. Each of the partners was essentially providing consulting services to the clientele on a staff augmentation basis, which allowed us to start to build up revenue and cash balances. In parallel, in the evenings, I would work on proposals to customers to enable them to sell people other than themselves. After approximately six months, we hired our first consultant, who is still with the operation today.

From there, we slowly built up a team of consultants while still being consultants ourselves, and our goal then became to deliver our own project for a customer—one that we could claim as our own reference, allowing us to market and promote our expertise as a project delivery business and not just a staff provider.

As you can imagine, at this stage, I was burning the candle at both ends, working full days with clients and then working on the business at night. And then, two and a half years from when we started, we won our first project. That was cause for great celebration as this was a key part of our strategy. We were finally morphing into a consultancy, or so we thought …

What we really morphed into was a cohort with a strong brand, which, from the outside, looked great. The business grew slowly but steadily to around 10 people. However, our cohort had an inherent growth-inhibiting flaw in its DNA, and progress was less than stellar due to slow growth in its particular niche (CRM had not yet taken off as it would a few years later) and a lack of proactive sales and marketing.

Sales at this point happened almost exclusively through existing relationships and word of mouth. We knew growth was necessary, so we hired our first salesperson. With more clients coming in, the company continued to grow to a team of around 16 people in its fifth year. That's when the crisis came.

A key client—at that stage more than 60 percent of our total revenue—was the subject of a hostile takeover. Overnight, the client cut their spend with us by 90 percent. The financial pressure for Bluleader was mounting, and I knew I had reached the end with my company. It felt like rather than having built a sustainable, growing enterprise, it was more of a roller-coasterride of ups and downs. I was planning to sell out to my partners for a relatively small amount.

Enter a man who I will refer to throughout this book as "Millionaire Mentor."

Millionaire Mentor was the founder of his own tech services firm—one he owned with a group of three others. Much like me, Millionaire Mentor had been highly successful in building his firm. Much like me, despite his success, he was still working long hours as the company's CEO. He and his co-founders made good profits but were not enjoying their lives. Not a single one of them.

Eventually, Millionaire Mentor decided to turn over his CEO responsibilities to the company's top salesperson, with the other founders following suit by stepping out of the day-to-day. This was all possible because the business had truly developed a life of its own. Another year and a half later, the founders sold the company all while keeping a competent management team intact.

The big question lingering in Millionaire Mentor's mind was "Is it possible to build a business as successful as mine and have a fulfilling private life at the same time?"

I connected with Millionaire Mentor soon before he sold his

business. When we first spoke, he identified with my situation 100 percent, empathizing with the idea of a quick, unprofitable exit. However, without hesitation, he challenged me not to take that path. Rather, he advised me that we work together to turn the whole thing around.

The objective was simple: Build an amazing, fast-growing tech services business and enjoy life … simultaneously. *As Tim Ferriss says, don't live a deferred life plan.* Don't work hard and drive yourself into the ground now so you can be rich and happy "someday."

During our coaching sessions, we focused on both my life and my business. I had to design a new lifestyle for my family and me. I had to hire people smarter than me. I had to get out of the weeds and focus on structuring and building the business. My goal was to transform Bluleader from a cohort to a real business and to transform myself from a contractor to a business leader.

As a result, five years after it launched, Bluleader became an incredibly strong brand—so much so that system integrators would refer to Bluleader as "the real prize" when it came to SAP CX services. The business grew rapidly to over 80 consultants, with a growth rate of more than 40 percent per year. In 2020, a global tech giant made an offer we could not refuse, so we sold. On the personal front, people I knew outside my business constantly commented on the number of overseas vacations we took as a family, not to mention the enjoyable international business trips.

What to Expect

The principles found here will turn your business "from sweat to scale," even if only 50 percent of them are done well. We never managed to achieve 100 percent in all of them at Bluleader, but progressively, quarter by quarter, by implementing quarterly anchors, the dial started to turn. We had reached the point of sustainable growth.

At the time of this writing, I have launched my next business. Through the research I have done for this book, I was able to reflect on my own journey, learn from people, who have done things better than me, and learn from the experiences of my coaching clients.

The world of tech services is a tough game until you know how to play it.

The Sweat2Scale approach to technology services scaling is what I call the "MATE Framework." This framework captures all the components required to scale your business.

The MATE Framework

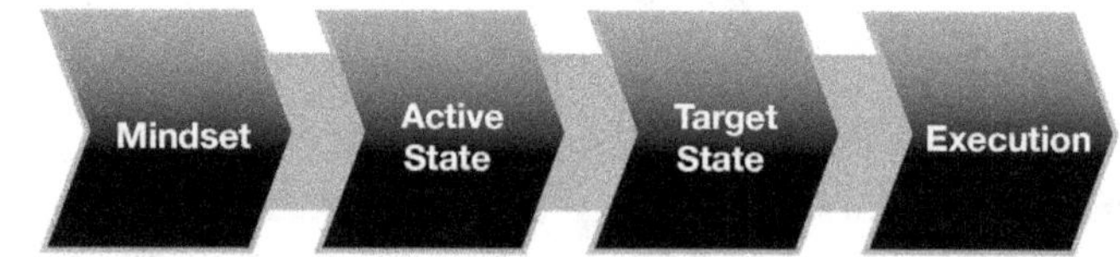

Mindset

To move from sweat to scale will first require some mindset changes. These include moving from a contractor to a business-owner mindset or from an employee to an independent mindset. For most, the main barrier to achieving these mindset shifts is remaining stagnant in a hands-on approach to project delivery.

As a leader and business owner, you are responsible for business development and other business functions. What many people do, however, is remain addicted to the revenue that their time can generate—they never fully empower their teams to work without their close involvement. This is not for malicious reasons but more about ensuring good cash flow. But it will hold you back. You must make the mindset shift to being a business owner instead of an individual contributor by hiring people better than you to deliver results. I call this "getting off the tools." Despite the risk of potentially upsetting some customers, without making this shift, progress will be either slow or nonexistent.

Active State

Once you have made the mindset shift, which incidentally will need to happen many times as you make step changes in the business journey, you need to define the active or current state of the business. This will help you to determine the many good things about the business, as well highlight areas for improvement that will need to be addressed.

Target State

Knowing your Active State, you can now look forward to defining your Target State. Where do you want the business to be in one, three, and five years? Think about how large the business will be in terms of revenue, profit, and people. You will also define what you want to be known for in your space and as a business.

Execution

Finally, once the Target State is clearly set, you can specify the steps to execution. This is a dynamic plan defined quarterly over the life of the business. The components of the execution plan will be known as "anchors," with owners and dates allocated to each anchor. These anchors will always be aligned to an engine that needs to be set up or tuned regularly.

Before we take a deep dive into the MATE Framework, I first want to explore the reasons for and benefits of growing your business and growing it fast. If you start with the end in mind, you are moving the odds massively in your favor to achieving success. There is hope for you! My framework will allow you to finally wipe the sweat from your brow and start to scale. Remember, your present and future selves are counting on it!

PART I

WHY GROW?

The Power of Growing Your Business

When Apple co-founder Steve Wozniak left Apple in 1985, he called it "the bane of his existence." He said he missed "the fun of the early days," believing the company had "been going in the wrong direction for the last five years."[2] He enjoyed the engineering aspect of the company over management. In short, he wanted to create a computer for hobbyists while Steve Jobs wanted to create something much bigger. Jobs clearly got his way, and Wozniak left.

Some co-founders of tech businesses identify with Wozniak more than with Jobs. Quite often, founders do not see eye to eye on this topic, which creates permanent tension. The bigger the gap, the greater the tension, and the more likely that the issues will quickly be driven to conclusion. If the tension is mild, though, things might not ever come to a head. As a result, it could plague the business for many years to come.

This section is about the debate between staying small and growing fast. If there is no such debate within yourself or among the other owners of your business—if you are all totally committed to the concept of fast growth—then skip this part.

For the purpose of this book, I'll define "staying small" as less than 10 percent growth and "growing fast" as 20 percent or more in growth.

As an example, a business that turns over $3 million today will turn over $24.5 million after eight years if it grows 30 percent year over year. If it chooses to stay small, though, let's say 5 percent growth year over year, it will turn over just $4.4 million after eight years—an astonishing difference.

So, who's better off? Some people might argue that the stay-small person is better off because they're having more fun, their marriage is still intact, and they've spent more time with their children. This position can be true if you're comparing it to a poorly executed fast-growth business option.

That is exactly what this book is about: to convince you that fast growth can indeed be easier than staying small if you execute properly. As a bonus, you can have a happy marriage and spend ample time with your children while you grow it!

We have determined that fast growth is highly desirable, but why would we focus on tech services? Surely it's much more scalable to build a technology product or software solution? We have all heard and seen the success stories of software solutions that have sold or are valued at multiple billions of dollars, and therefore, we are instantly drawn to this as a sure way to build success. I am not saying that this is not true, but there are a number of reasons why a tech services business is an attractive and lucrative alternative option.

In the next chapter, we'll explore the benefits of owning not just a tech services firm but one that grows lightning fast and why there is a high demand for these types of businesses in the tech space.

CHAPTER 3

The Benefits of Owning a Fast-Growing Tech Services Firm

The media tends to focus heavily on software acquisitions, but constant mergers and acquisitions are going on in the professional services sector as well.

The fact is that massive companies have a mechanism whereby they regularly acquire smaller tech services not just any firms. They target ones that have established at least 25 percent growth, year over year, for at least three years running. This has been the trend—the standard—for 30 years, and there are no signs of it stopping. (Over the last five years in the USA, there has been an average of 5,000 mergers and acquisitions transactions with an average total value of $225 billion per year in the professional services industry.[3])

A large company stops growing organically at a certain point, which is why they need smaller companies with proven consistent growth to help them move into new environments. In short, there is good money to be made in professional services.

That's exciting, isn't it? Why? Because your tech services firm has the potential to be in that position if you follow the MATE Framework outlined in this book.

If that's not enough to convince you of the benefits of owning a fast-growing tech services firm, then take a look at the growth statistics, which are accurate at the time of writing.

According to the International Trade Administration, "digitally delivered services account for more than 50 percent of US services trade and 20 percent of all US exports. Additionally, data flows account for at least 2.4 million US jobs."[4] Between 2014 and 2019, the industry grew at an average annual rate of 4.2 percent.[5] Additionally, Analysys Mason, the world's leading management consultancy focused on telecoms, media, and technology (TMT), predicts IT spending by small- and medium-size businesses (SMBs) will grow at a compound annual growth rate of 7.5 percent between 2022 and 2027.

"Cloud-based services will drive this growth because they support a distributed workforce, improve efficiency, and provide business resiliency," *ChannelVision Magazine* reported. "SMB IT spending on cloud-based categories is expected to grow from $600 billion in 2022 to $1 trillion in 2027."[6]

Skills gaps, wage inflation, and the war for talent will push CIOs to rely more on consultancies and managed services firms to pursue their digital strategies, according to tech research and consulting firm Gartner.

"Gartner expects the vast majority of large organizations to use external consultants to develop their cloud strategy over the next few years."[7]

I've been working in this industry for more than 25 years, and every time new technology comes out, vendors say they'll simplify things for you and you won't need consultants anymore. That is a myth. Vendors do not eliminate the need for consultants.

For example, the cloud was supposed to get rid of consulting firms, but it actually increased the need for more of them. Similarly, when SAP came out, you got an off-the-shelf ERP system and were told there was no longer a need for developers. That wasn't true either. In reality, people started using the tool to create a high-value extension to the off-the-shelf solution. You buy this solution and implement the system, but the people who knew how to configure it were paid double the amount of money as developers. This all created a massive services market.

For every dollar spent by a customer on licenses, they will spend at least $2–$3 on services.[8]

Why does the amount spent on services increase over time? Because people get better bang for their buck. Before ERP, a developer would receive $100,000 to create 100 screens. Now, you have an SAP developer who can create 1,000 screens at the same value. A business sees that value in both the software and the consultant.

Every evolution I've seen simply moved the previous effort into other areas, such as cybersecurity, cloud migrations, integration, etc. Therefore, the perceived threat to services has in fact caused the growth of more services. Additional drivers of more services in the near future will be

- COVID 19, which has driven remote working technologies,

- the need to understand how to "sweat" existing assets without purchasing more software,

- high returns on investments through productivity improvements from the power of new software, meaning companies will be able to spend more on services,

- exponential growth of cybersecurity requirements, and

- the move to hybrid deployment models, such as cloud and on-premise software, creating many service opportunities in integration, data sharing, etc.

It is clear that there is a high need—and therefore a great business opportunity—for tech services.

Tech services companies require far less up-front capital than product development businesses. They also start generating cash much sooner than product businesses do. If managed well, these businesses can be a much lower-risk option than a product development company.

Additionally, the model suits a technology practitioner very well. You can start incrementally by selling your skills to customers and, over time, scaling to transition over to people in the team you build. As you have the skills, you know how to hire and what "good" looks like. The challenge, of course, is to build the team in such a way that you are no longer the top consultant on the team.

All of this is to say that you are in a good place, because there will always be a need for tech services. This means there is a proven path to reach your financial goals if you structure your business properly. For these reasons, I believe—and have proven—that a well-structured tech services business can provide a great place to work for vast financial rewards as well as offer a fulfilling lifestyle for you and the ones you love.

Now, in the back of your mind, you may be asking, "Marco, this all sounds well and good, but where do I even begin?"

You'd think the obvious answer is to earn more business as fast as possible; however, the true starting point is at the very end. In the next chapter, I'll go over exactly how to plan for your grand exit. Not only will this create a vision for the framework that follows, but it will also get you excited at the thought of a better future.

CHAPTER 4

Start with the End in Mind

Why think about the end of your journey with your business at all? You want to see success with your sales and operations. You want to be highly profitable. Why would you want to leave?

I've been through the process of imagining what the end looks like for tech services entrepreneurs countless times. Every time I do, the immediate results are almost as satisfying as the eventual outcome (achieving the dream). In two very recent cases, I've seen an instant transformation of both mindset and attitude.

For one of my clients, thinking about the end goal has pushed them to have a laser focus on the day-to-day operation of the business and given them hope for the future. When they first started working with me, they looked tired. Now they're bright eyed and salivating at the prospect of growing beyond their wildest dreams.

In another case, my client's business has grown fourfold over the past year because we worked to identify his end goal! He tells me that every time he feels low, thinking about the end goal is what keeps him going.

Starting with the end in mind makes the day-to-day a lot more bearable. A lot of tech services business owners never think of an exit. They are tired and worn out. I was one of those guys.

The first meeting that Bluleader's board had with Millionaire Mentor was the start of a very interesting journey. After initial introductions, he walked up to the whiteboard and asked the question, "So what is the exit strategy?"

To be honest, up to this point, five years in, I had never considered this question. I had always assumed we would just keep running the business ad infinitum, ensuring we made good cash flow along the way.

According to business guru Tony Robbins, "87 percent of all businesses will never be sold, because the person didn't know what they were doing. Most people don't run their business in a way where they can legitimately sell it, they have no exit strategy, and they'll go away. It will make you run your business differently if you run it where it's possible to sell it. If you don't, you're going to run it like something that's not a business, and you'll never grow anything. Without an exit strategy, all you have is a job. An expensive job. A job with a lot of responsibility, a job with a lot of risk. You call it a business, but without an exit strategy, it's not. The purpose of a business is to build a system that can make money when you're not there, and if done right, you can sell the business for a multiple."[9]

When you get to a certain size, your business becomes a hamster wheel. Every year is the same. Most people who start businesses need something to work toward, but when you get into the routine of running a business, even when it's doing well, it can become mundane. You ask, "Where is this all going?" Your co-workers say, "We're making money, but so what? I don't even have time to go on vacation."

I instantly noticed how my approach and behavior changed once we had defined our exit plan, which was to drive toward a trade sale. Once I started to run my business as if I were going to sell it (even if those were not my immediate plans), we operated differently. Our recordkeeping became more organized. We started systemizing, making the business less dependent on the owners. We became much more focused on how we were building value into the business. This simple action of locking in an exit strategy had an immediate positive impact.

Trade Sale

Before crafting an exit strategy, you first must understand the different mechanisms for exit. The most common is positioning your business to be a desirable target for a trade sale, otherwise known as selling to another business via acquisition, which can be very profitable for tech services companies.

Businesses buy other businesses for all types of reasons. They might want to use a new acquisition as a quick path to expansion, realize synergies from complementary business activities, or simply buy out (and get rid of) the competition.

Advantage of a Trade Sale

- A competing business may be highly motivated to purchase your business, making for a quick sale and maximum profit. For stock market–listed potential buyers, your earnings before interest and tax (EBIT) will potentially add much value to their business if they are trading at a strong price-earnings (P/E) ratio, e.g., they might buy your business at six times EBIT, but they are trading at a P/E ratio of 10. Therefore, your EBIT will have an immediate net improvement on their business value.

Disadvantages of a Trade Sale

- If the purchaser's only motivation is to reduce the competition, they may fold your business after purchase. As a result, existing employees may lose their jobs.

- A competitor may only pretend to be interested in purchasing your business to gain access to your confidential business information. That's why listing your business for sale confidentially with a business broker is a smart choice. They will require any firm with inquiries on your business to sign a nondisclosure agreement(NDA) and will prescreen potential buyers as much as possible before they get their hands on any confidential information.

If one or more of the owners is uncomfortable with the discussion around the exit strategy, i.e., they don't want to think about selling their baby, then give it some time and bring back the discussion at a later stage. If it's you who is hesitant, don't think of it as a problem but as an opportunity. A reluctant seller could drive the sell price up in more ways than you might think, and their averseness to sell could translate into new goals and aspirations.

For example, an obvious question to the co-owner who opposes an exit strategy might be "If the thought of selling the business is unbearable to you, what would make it worthwhile?" The answer might be more money, that she wants to keep her job, or that she wants to keep the brand alive. Whatever her answer, it could potentially become a condition of the exit.

At Bluleader, one of the co-owners needed more money to make it worthwhile. He also wanted to play golf every Wednesday and for our staff to work for a company that treats its employees fairly. So, we increased our asking price and put a plan in place to achieve it. His Wednesday golf became an "unwritten" condition of the trade sale, and we limited the list of potential buyers to companies that treat their staff well.

The short version of the story is a reluctant seller is an opportunity for better outcomes.

While a trade sale is the most common exit mechanism, there are alternatives, detailed below. Don't be overwhelmed by these. If a trade sale is most appealing to you, skip to the end of this chapter.

Sell the Business on the Open Market

This is the most popular exit mechanism option for small businesses (turning less than $3 million in revenue), and it's not typically suitable for tech services firms but more akin to how your uncle may sell his restaurant, for example. At a point in time, often when the owner is ready to retire, the business is put up for sale at a certain price—in the hope that the owner walks away with a good amount of money for all his hard work.

Advantages

- A profitable business should be attractive to buyers.

- Assets and owner benefits are incorporated when valuing the business for sale, maximizing the return to the owner.

Disadvantages

- A marginally profitable business can be very difficult to sell.

- Finding a buyer on the open market can be a long process.

Keep Your Business in the Family

This is the dream of many business owners. It ensures that your legacy lives on and provides a living for your heirs.

Advantages

- A family business can make for a smooth transition by grooming a family successor.

- A family business may allow you to keep a hand in the business in an advisory (or other) capacity.

Disadvantages

- Developing a family succession plan can be enormously difficult. Sometimes it can lead to discord among family members over ownership and/or participation in the business.

- Family members may not have the skills or interest to take over the business.

IPO

Listing a company on the stock market is another option that can provide a lucrative exit from the business. Listed companies must go through a rigorous due diligence process before they can be listed on the stock exchange. Due to the costs and effort involved, this will typically be more suited to a larger business, i.e., greater than $50 million in revenue.

Advantages

- An IPO creates a market valuation for the business and the opportunity to raise capital for expansion as well as the possibility of realizing some of your investment.

- An IPO provides access to an acquisition currency and transparency around the value of the business. Listed companies often use their shares, as opposed to cash, to make acquisitions. This can be particularly useful when implementing a buy-and-build strategy when cash can be better utilized in other areas.

- It encourages employee commitment by rewarding them with something of clear value—they can see exactly what their shares or options are worth. When there's no objective market valuation or ability to buy or sell shares—as is normally the case in a private company—it can be difficult for employees with shares or options to understand the value they have been given.

- It creates a heightened public profile and improves the ability to attract high-caliber board members.

- It improves supplier, investor, and customer confidence and elevates your standing in the marketplace. This can help enormously if you're trying to build a global business.

Disadvantages

- IPOs increase external accountability and scrutiny. Public companies are public property. As such, they are expected to comply with the rules of the markets they populate.

- There is a risk of undervaluation of the business in an IPO. Issuing shares is not only dilutive, but shares can also lack liquidity. This can undermine fundraising and acquisition activity due to a lack of demand for the shares. In addition, a lack of demand normally translates into a low share price, so the use of shares as an acquisition currency may also lose its appeal. On the public markets, companies' share prices are not only affected by their own performance but by the performance of the market and the economy as a whole.

Sell Partially to a Wealthy Individual or Private Equity (PE) Firm

For these entities, a stake in a technology services business is treated as an investment opportunity with a targeted outcome or exit, e.g., grow the value of the business and sell at a later stage with a good return on investment. Depending on the size of the acquired stake, these buyers will seek a position on the board of the company to ensure their desired outcomes.

Advantages

- This strategy can turbocharge the business due to a potential cash injection and strategic insight.

- It allows current shareholders to partially cash in on their efforts to date but still allows for upside in the future.

- It can provide more learning and networking opportunities for the current directors, thanks to access to sophisticated investors.

- It has the potential to provide access to high-quality clients via the networks of the PE or wealthy individual.

Disadvantages

- This strategy can cause company culture to suffer if the business becomes a purely investment-driven venture.

- It may result in company direction being taken off track if the investors have little or no understanding of your business.

- It can prolong the exit, which can be a negative for those wanting to exit quickly.

Sell to a Co-Founder

It is not uncommon for shareholders to sell their shares to one another as a means of creating an exit. This can occur when there is a difference in economic position between the shareholders or company direction. Sometimes, one shareholder might be looking to exit, but the others are not. This then becomes a very good option and should be included up front in a shareholders' agreement. Normally, the agreement will detail the terms of the share purchase, e.g., valuation method, payment terms, and competitive restraints. If this is not already detailed, a negotiation will be required.

Advantages

- This approach allows the strategy to remain intact due to maintaining the same leadership.

- It is a rapid method of exit.

- It allows for easier decision-making.

Disadvantages

- It can create conflict if terms have not been pre-agreed.

- It may confuse the market or employees if the existing shareholder is well known.

- It could negatively impact sales numbers and escalations if the shareholder is at the center of everything.

Break Down the Goal

Once Bluleader had determined what our exit mechanism was, we then started the process of working backward to see how this would look over a period of time. This process looks something like this:

1. What would each shareholder like to walk away with at the end? What should be the after-tax amount?

2. What does that mean in terms of a final acquisition amount?

3. What are typical multiples of either revenue or EBIT in your industry on an acquisition?

4. Now define your target EBIT or revenue. Break down a time-based road map from where your business is now to the target. How does this translate into numbers of staff, customers, and revenue streams?

5. What other nonfinancial metrics will draw in a buyer? It's critical to be networking with industry peers to try and glean as much of this information as possible. These metrics can then be built into your business.

6. What will the organization structure look like at the time of the trade sale, and how will the team or practice achieve the revenue targets? The overall revenue target will seem daunting, but when you study revenue targets at the team level, suddenly, it all feels achievable.

Understanding Earnouts

For many acquisitions, the buyer will want the owners who are running the business to remain for a certain period of time to assist with assimilation and drive growth. They will tie financial rewards, which are part of the valuation of the business, to meeting goals within that period. So, for example, they might say they are buying the business for $10 million, but 20 percent of that will be paid at the end of the agreed period. This is known as an "earnout period."

It's important to determine whether the owners will want to be part of an earnout, as this means becoming an employee all over again. For many, this makes the earnout particularly challenging due to having less autonomy and being under more financial pressure (as not everyone gets a bite of the cherry).

Most acquisitions will incorporate an earnout with financial golden handcuffs, but if owners do not want that, they need to structure the business in such a way that this is not required. This entails a clear handover to a management team, incentive plans for that team, and potentially taking less from the sale proceeds. Therefore, factoring this in up front will aid in determining the final target sale amount.

The power of the earnout is in having a clear goal to work toward. It's all about planting the seed and nurturing it as it grows.

So, now that you have the exit mechanisms, we will conclude this chapter by returning to the Millionaire Mentor's question with which we started: "What is the exit strategy?" Take out a pen and paper, open up your note-taking app, or grab a marker and head to a whiteboard. You'll want to answer the questions below in order to determine your exit strategy:

- Do you want to exit?

- For how much do you want to sell the business?

- What are your criteria for selling (time frame and/or revenue goal)?

- Will you use a broker?

- Which exit mechanism are you going to use?

- Do you want an earnout?

If this all becomes too overwhelming for you, just imagine training like an Olympian every day without actually having the goal of going to the Olympics. After years of consistent hard work, you're surely good enough to win a gold medal. So, aim for gold at the Olympics! Suddenly, that tiring, boring daily training gives you purpose. And when you have purpose, you are more likely to set—and stay focused on—a path to victory!

Now you have a clear view of what the end goal may look like for you. At this point in the game, it's advisable to do your due diligence and question if the approach you've chosen is the right one. To drive the point home even further, the next chapter discusses the various myths about business growth that may stand in the way of execution.

CHAPTER 5

Dispelling Myths

We've been through the benefits of owning a fast-growing business, so what might still be stopping you from going for it? Those pesky thoughts in the back of your mind telling you to just stay small because it's safe? Some would label them "limiting beliefs." Others would call it "rationalizing." However, let's call a spade a spade: these are myths.

Below, I'll dissect the common myths about growing a business to better equip you as you head into the first portion of the MATE Framework in part II: Mindset.

Myth 1: A Small Business Is More Fun

Babies and toddlers are fun, right? But how would you feel if your toddler does not grow up like other children? If she wears nappies forever, if she throws tantrums on the supermarket floor at age 25, and if she never learns to read and write.

A 10-year-old small business is not the same as a new small business. If the idea of a new small business translates to feelings of excitement and novelty, then the idea of an old small business translates to something very different.

In an old small business, in my experience, the main source of excitement is the customer—the hope that the next customer will bring some novelty into our lives and present us with a problem we find interesting. However, even such novelties wear off, and eventually, we find ourselves yawning at any new challenge thrown to us by our customers.

Okay, so the first point here is that a small business can seem like more fun but only if it is new.

The second point is this: The perception of fun only happens in retrospect. It's like climbing a steep mountain. Think about it. What do you actually enjoy? Is it the muscle pain, the blisters, the rain, the slippery rocks, or the fear of death? No, you don't enjoy any of that, but when you look back afterward, you say, "That was fun! When can we do it again?"

If Steve Wozniak wants to build computers in his garage again, he can do that anytime. But he doesn't because it won't be the same as the first time.

Myth 2: A Fast-Growing Business Is Painful

When Millionaire Mentor came to Bluleader, I was only thinking about survival. I was not considering growth. Many view the idea of growing a business fast an unpleasant journey. People truly believe growth will be painful and having a bigger company will lead to more headaches.

This is the main objective of this book: to offer a road map for fast growth that is less painful than staying small.

While I cannot condense the entire book down into one paragraph, I can offer a key message here: A growing business is a natural phenomenon and is easier to manage than a business that does not grow. Raising a baby that grows ½ inch to 1 inch per month, which is the norm,[10] is easier than raising a baby that doesn't grow. We nurture babies, and we anticipate their growth. If we nurture our business (for growth) and if we anticipate growth, it will happen, and it will feel normal.

Will it be free of pain? No, there will be pain. But a small business that doesn't grow has pain of a different kind. To have no business at all has pain of its own. To have children is painful. To grow old without children is painful in its own way. Choose which pain you will bear.

Myth 3: A Large Business Is Less Innovative

A large business can be more innovative than a small business. Jeff Bezos has illustrated this by structuring teams within his business that follow his two-pizza rule. He argues that smaller teams are more innovative, so his rule is if a team is not small enough that it can be fed with two pizzas, the team needs to be broken up into smaller teams so that innovation can continue to happen.[11] This simple rule is considered by many as the secret to his success. Jeff Bezos basically provides evidence that if leaders value innovation, they will find a way to preserve it in a growing business.

Myth 4: A Large Business Has Too Many Rules

A large business will typically have more rules, and as entrepreneurs, we hate rules, right? Even if the rules are allowed to accumulate gradually and are kept under control, we consider this the norm.

But is it really a problem? Employees will only think so if their perceived freedom is under threat, and freedom is an interesting thing. More than 50 percent of US citizens do not have passports—out of choice![12] However, these people still consider themselves free, as they have more than sufficient space to move around. If the USA was the size of the world's smallest country, Vatican City (110 acres), they would feel different.

Give your employees enough space to move around.

In a large company, employees might not have the freedom to buy their own laptops and get reimbursed, but they have other kinds of freedom: more career options, more staff who can step in when they go on leave, more parental leave, an unlimited budget for buying e-books, etc. The benefits that come with growth in a large business can actually increase the level of perceived freedom.

Myth 5: A Large Business Is Less Spontaneous

When you're steering a large boat, you cannot drive it like a Ferrari. Decisions need to be made more thoroughly, and all the major parties need to be on board. The business might have a board of directors that gives direction to the CEO, who then formulates an execution plan for the management team, etc.

However, the spontaneous culture will continue to exist if the owners make it a priority. Break the business down into smaller teams, and give them as much autonomy as possible. Give each team leader freedom in execution as well as a budget for innovation and entertainment, even if it's small. Let teams go out and have fun on their own terms. If they blow their entire entertainment budget in one evening, then let it be.

Myth 6: A Large Business Is Less Personal

This is only true if there are no thriving subcultures in the business. If the only interaction employees have with the company is a quarterly webinar where the CEO broadcasts her view of the world, then the experience is very impersonal indeed.

However, if the company has strong subcultures within the teams, who cares about the CEO or the founders? Keep breaking the company down into smaller teams, encourage personal relationships at the team level, and check the pulse regularly.

Myth 7: A Fast-Growing Business Requires Longer Working Hours

This is simply not true. Working hours are a choice.

The working hours of a business are more closely related to its culture and market position than the pace of growth. A business that is not niche, and is poorly positioned in the market, needs its staff to work long hours just to stay ahead, which then engenders a culture of long working hours.

In the IT services space, we have seen companies that work long hours and others that don't, and there's no visible correlation with success or growth. With smart hiring and delegation, this myth can be busted!

Myth 8: A Small Business Is Easier Than a Large Business

I'm making a case for the opposite. A large business is easier. Ask any tech services entrepreneur who grew a large business with hundreds of employees, sold it, and then started over again. Ask that same person if it's easy to be small. Do not be surprised if they say it is very hard.

How can anyone argue that DIY is easier than delegating to competent staff? Going from owning a big company back to a small one is the equivalent of a Formula 1 driver stepping out of a Formula 1 car and climbing back into a go-cart. While it's easier for a beginner to drive the go-cart, once you know how to drive the Formula 1 car, it will certainly become your preference.

Few people are as committed to growth as somebody who stepped out of a large business into a small one. They know how much easier it is to run a bigger business, and like so many things in life, it's only easy once you know how to do it.

So, there you have it. All myths debunked. Time to move on and get started. There are three concepts in the next chapter that are really going to kick your motivation into high gear. With these elements swirling through your head as you go on this journey, it will be easier to remain motivated and focused on reaching your end goal.

CHAPTER 6

Novelty, Growth, and Hope

Before we explore the MATE Framework, here are some important factors to consider. Three things make a business enjoyable:

- Novelty

- Growth

- Hope of future achievement

All three bring joy to your world, and all three are present in a successful start-up.

Novelty

Researchers have found that novelty releases dopamine in the brain.[13] While many people are happy to work in a business that stays the same, our natural desire is to experience novelty and to anticipate a regular supply of future novelty. I'm not saying you should be chasing dopamine hits by paying the ultimate sacrifice of losing focus of your direction. My argument is rather that you should step out of your comfort zone regularly and, in doing so, move the business up a level.

Growth

Think about how much older people love gardens and babies. It may be that elderly people struggle to find growth in themselves, but nothing stops them from enjoying the growth of plants and humans. They are not alone in this. We all love growth—whether you're an entrepreneur or an employee, we love to somehow be part of something that grows.

Hope of Future Achievement

Pioneer of the self-help movement Napoleon Hill argued that the "hope of future achievement" is one of the key ingredients of a happy life.[14] Note with great benefit that the hope of achievement rates higher than the achievement itself. It rates higher even than the concept of financial freedom.

Now, think about your own business. All three of these things were present when it was a new business, but if it stops growing, they all disappear. You're left with very little novelty, no growth, and little hope of future achievement.

A growing business, on the other hand, challenges you to step out of your comfort zone and into the world of novelty and growth, and by setting aggressive growth targets, you always have the hope of future achievement.

David Shein, founder of Com Tech Communications (arguably Australia's first tech unicorn) and author of *The Dumbest Guy at the Table*, has said that in order to feel happy, we must have someone to love, something to do, and something to look forward to. Further, Robin Sharma, one of the world's top leadership experts and best-selling author, says, "We are all here for some special reason. Stop being a prisoner of your past. Become the architect of your future."[15]

Therefore, your greatest achievement lies in the future, not the past.

Set yourself some aggressive growth targets, learn the skills of growth, and give your mental health a boost. All of this and more are discussed in detail in the section that follows, which is all about setting yourself up for future achievement through beneficial mindset practices.

PART II
MINDSET

CHAPTER 7

Paradigm Transformation

Many business books focus on what you can *do*. They give you nearly endless strategies and tactics. But more often than not, this may lead to you spinning your wheels.

Why? Because you have not changed your mindset before trying to implement unfamiliar strategies. Before you can *do* anything, it's important to evaluate the way you think.

Mindset is both the key enabler and the leading hand brake for success. If your mindset as an owner is misaligned, the business will constantly seem as if it's not building momentum. So, again, the first step toward scaling is to get your mind right.

What are key mindset challenges and opportunities you will face as an owner?

I Am the Best at What We Do in the Company

This is a very common view held by owners of professional services businesses. They either started their business as a contractor who was at the top of their game or were the top salesperson in their field. These are great attributes to have when starting out but become a hindrance as the business grows.

For scale to occur, you must let go of the status that comes with being the best. Instead, find others who can take tasks away from you. Once you do, you will come to realize that someone completely focused on a task will always end up doing a better job than you, as you simply cannot focus in the same way given all your other responsibilities. To shift to this mindset, we apply the Triple A principle:

A = Aptitude; A = Affability; A = Availability

If you do high-quality work for a client, you will score 10/10 for Aptitude, 10/10 for Affability (hopefully!), but only 2/10 for Availability (as you are so busy on the business). This gives you a score of 22/30 for your work.

If you can delegate to someone who might not be as good as you at the task but is good with people, he might score 7/10 for Aptitude, 10/10 for Affability, and 10/10 for Availability. His work score is 27/30; therefore, your client will be much happier with the performance of your business.

One of my clients, a managing director at his firm, experienced this when I explained the Triple A principle to him. He decided to delegate the client-facing activities he had been handling to one of his junior employees who was more available. At first, this concerned him because the staff member might do a bad job and upset the client. However, to his surprise, his customer raved about the junior person, as he was so responsive to said customer.

I Can Grow the Business Without Investment

Some business owners, depending on factors such as upbringing or attitudes toward money, do not view spending on business for growth as an investment. However, traditional direct money injection is not the only way to invest. For example, you could also give up certain revenue streams to focus on higher-value business activities or return your focus to the core of the business. This will come at a short-term cost, but in the long run, like any investment, it will yield higher returns.

To Grow, We Need to Move Out of Our Niche and Diversify

This is a great temptation when you are smaller. If you have assessed that the niche, as a market, is in fact large enough, then stick to the niche. I'll talk later about why, but suffice to say, scale becomes easier if you can focus on a niche. For example, a customer of mine has found that by narrowing his focus (cybersecurity) to cybersecurity for Amazon Web Services Cloud (AWS), he is experiencing substantial growth as well as higher staff satisfaction.

If a market is big enough, and you decide you're going to own it (by being a well-known expert), you will find you experience much more rapid growth, because the niche supports you. In the example above, AWS brings business to my client, because he's "the guy." His staff is satisfied because they know what they need to do and know how to do it well. Conversely, if he decided to change up what his staff did on a quarterly basis, they'd always feel as if they were behind the eight ball.

If I Am Not Busy, We Are Not Productive

As you become a larger business, your busyness will not be on everyday work activities but rather on setting up strategies or hiring the correct key people and giving them the leadership that allows them to succeed. This means you will need to change how you view being busy.

There might be stages where you are not "doing" much but instead focus on high-yielding activities that don't necessarily take too long, such as making a critical phone call to close a deal or having dinner with your next practice manager.

Growth Is a Burden

I have been working with a husband–wife team with a staff of about 40 employees. In an early conversation with these entrepreneurs, the husband, CEO of the company, said to me, "I almost regret that we've grown so much. Maybe we should go backward and be smaller again."

There's something better out there than simply surviving. It is possible to grow fast and not feel like the couple in this example. Remember, you need that novelty, growth, and hope for future achievement that we discussed in the previous section to be your driving forces. Growth should not become a burden. If it is, you are doing something wrong.

This part of the book will look at how we can create a scale mindset in your business. Remember, starting with the end in mind is your North Star. I briefly touched on the idea of you relinquishing control of being the best in your business. The point I want to drive home here is that **you must transform your mindset from being a techie who puts food on the table for your family to a businessperson who looks at the bigger picture.**

So, let's go further into how you do that using key concepts and strategies that will get you backing off the tools. You are no longer the team captain, no longer a player–coach. You will build a culture that enriches your team and gets you to a place where everyone's vision is aligned, executing your strategy and working toward a common goal.

Key Takeaways

1. Mindset is both the main enabler and the leading hand brake for success. Before implementing unfamiliar strategies, you must evaluate the way you think.

2. For scale to occur, you need to let go of the status that comes with being the best and find others who can take tasks away from you. Remember the Triple A principle: Aptitude, Affability, and Availability.

3. Key mindset focus areas are

    a. having an investment mindset,

    b. having a niche and sticking to it,

    c. being busy with strategy, and

    d. determining for yourself whether you see growth as a burden or a blessing.

CHAPTER 8

You Are No Longer the Best

You started your tech services company because you were likely the top consultant or salesperson in your field/industry. You're proud of what you've achieved. You're proud of the fact that you're at the top of your game—and you should be.

But now, it's time to move on to your next phase.

There are typically two phases that occur when you're first starting out at the helm of your business:

- **Phase 1:** You realize selling is more important than delivering, so you become good at selling. You're finally off the tools, and you've moved on to focus on growing your business through client acquisition.

- **Phase 2:** A new problem presents itself. You've gotten so good at selling that you're now the best salesperson at your company. You realize you either need to hire people who are better salespersons than you or you need to train and develop your existing staff to achieve the same result.

One caveat to note is that some people jump into sales at the start of their careers. So, that's one less step to worry about in this process. However, if this is you, and you've never been on the tools, that doesn't mean you're off the hook. You just start at a different level.

I went through both these stages myself. The problem is that being the best at anything other than leading eventually becomes a hindrance to scaling your business. If you're the best salesperson in the business, your business can't scale because it's totally reliant on you.

That's why, if you want to grow sustainably, you need to pass that mantle on to others within your team. If the best people aren't on your team yet, you must recruit equally qualified people—individuals in your niche who are better than you. From there, you must grow your team to overtake you in all areas, and that should be one of the crowning achievements within your company.

If you take anything away from this section on mindset, it should be this: *moving away from being the best is the single most important mindset shift you can make for the greatest impact on your business.*

But being able to make that shift from selling yourself to clients to selling your business to them is not always intuitive. It doesn't come naturally.

Eventually, it becomes extremely difficult because, as you're trying to focus on selling more work, you're also trying to hire people and work with internal and operational issues, all while aiming to provide a high-quality service to your customers … by yourself. It becomes exhausting, and you feel trapped because, more than just wanting your business, your customers want *you*.

David Shein attributes his success to the very concept of hiring people smarter than him and training them to take on his day-to-day responsibilities effectively. Having sold his company for an enterprise value of more than $1 billion, Shein encourages you, as the business owner of your tech services company, to transform into "the dumbest guy at the table."

Shein's concept is not new. In fact, pharmaceutical entrepreneur Ewing Marion Kauffman points out that by hiring people more astute than you, you compel the capabilities of your company to grow. Since these individuals are noticeably smarter (even if you hate to admit it), you are more likely to listen to their thoughts and ideas, which is the best way to expand your own capabilities and strengthen your company.[16]

Professionals take much pride in being the best at what they do. That accolade is, after all, what they have been pursuing for years. So, it's understandable that ego may come into play. Zeynep Ilgaz, co-founder of Confirm Biosciences, relates.

"Early in my career, I was hesitant to hire people I thought were smarter than me… Believe it or not, I had a bit of an ego. I didn't want to accept that I might not be the smartest person in the room. I feared losing respect; I thought that, as the leader, I should have all the answers."[17]

This sentiment is shared among some of the smartest and best businesspeople in the world, such as Michael Dell, CEO of Dell Technologies, and Guy Kawasaki, previously an employee of Apple and originally responsible for marketing the Macintosh computer line in 1984.

Avoid the idea of the fallback plan. Don't tell yourself that if the business doesn't work out, you can always go back to the tools and return to being an individual contributor. This is not an option. As a business owner, you're all in.

To achieve the prestige of being the dumbest guy at the table, evaluate what will be the best use of your time and skills and double down on that—go from being the best salesperson to meeting client executives and having laser focus on leading your direct reports and inspiring them to greatness. Invest in your team by focusing on training, shadowing, and mentorship. People we developed in this manner became some of our most loyal and dedicated team members.

Once you get to this point, congratulations! You just moved through phases 1 and 2. You are officially the dumbest person in the room. Now it's time to give the glory away. Meaning that even if you are in the process of training this exceptional new staff to take over your responsibilities, you're still involved in the day-to-day, and you have to credit your team for the business's triumphs. For example, if you were the person behind closing a deal, but a junior salesperson you were mentoring was involved in negotiations, make sure she gets the credit.

The more you pay credit to your staff in front of the customer and in front of their peers, the more everyone will believe in your operation (and themselves).

In the next chapter, I'll explain exactly how to make the transformation from being on the tools and being your customer's most reliable resource to leading a team of rockstars who, eventually, will do it better than you ever could.

Key Takeaways

1. The single most important mindset shift you can make for the greatest impact on your business is moving away from being the best.

2. If the best people aren't on your team yet, recruit equally qualified people to be individual contributors, and train them to overtake you in all areas.

3. Focus on leading your direct reports, inspiring them to greatness, and providing mentorship.

4. Once you get to this point, give the glory away.

CHAPTER 9

Transitioning from Team Captain to Army General

You've gotten past the first two phases of transitioning from the smartest person in the room to the dumbest person at the table. In other words, once you've mastered sales, it's time to move on to being a true leader.

However, we're not done yet. To be a business owner who effectively scales and grows his business with an end goal in mind, you must now move on to phase 3: alienating the position of player–coach, or team captain, and becoming the general of your army.

The captain of an elite soccer team has likely earned that title through being the best player with the club, a title he would normally hold for a number of years. Once his game deteriorates, however, the manager tells him, "Your match play has been suffering. I'm going to move you out of the captain role." If he is no longer the best, he can no longer be the leader.

This applies at all levels of the game and in every walk of life—from high school all the way to the top. The kids who excel in academics and in sports are appointed leadership positions. We are programmed to believe we have to be the best to be a leader.

However, in the real world, it doesn't quite work that way, especially in business.

A business is like a sports team, but you can enlist as many players as you want. Imagine growing your team to up to 50 players and playing against other teams that only have 12 players. Do you think the team with 50 players or the team with 12 players will perform better? Twelve is easier to manage than 50, right? The more players you have, the harder it gets, especially when you've been playing on the team for your entire career and have never actually led it.

Let's look at a few other examples of how this works in the real world. The soldier who becomes the army general and still operates like a soldier will never understand how to strategically win in battle. The teacher who becomes a principal and still operates like a teacher will never understand how to run a school—managing personalities of children, teachers, parents, administrative staff, and support staff—to make that school the very best it can be.

If you want to do something huge, you have to stop operating like a team captain, like a soldier, or like a high school teacher. Instead, you must operate like a manager, like a general, or like a principal. Lay down your weapons (your tools), and use your words of influence, your compassion for people, and your desire to help others to lead your team to victory in every battle you face.

David Shein built his company and sold it within 14 years. One of the reasons he was successfully able to do that was that in the first few months, he realized he wasn't a technical guy, and despite his background in accounting, he wasn't a good accountant. The only thing he knew he could do well was sell. So, he immediately hired the best technical people and an incredible accountant.

What Shein was doing throughout that process was reinventing himself. He dove straight into the role of army general and did it very quickly. A lot of companies take five to 10 years to come to that realization. Bluleader was one of those companies.

Shein's key message in all of this is that you, as the business owner, have one responsibility: your relationships with people. Those people include employees, customers, suppliers, and shareholders. Master that and you're truly at the top of the game.

One of my clients was the best at his technology skill when I started working with him. He had a small team but was still one of the players. He had to transition his approach from the role of captain to seeing himself as the leader—army general—who controls the strategy of the business. This process has taken him some time, but he is now in a position where he has a highly competent leadership team that has been able to take many tasks away from him. He recently said to me, "Hiring people I can delegate to has become addictive. I can see how we will reach our goals now. Before, I could not see it."

The key to making this transition is the mindset shift I've spoken of ad nauseam to this point. I've seen many new business owners start running their companies without changing their mindsets.

They haven't reinvented themselves. They haven't changed their job titles on LinkedIn. They still refer to themselves in conversations as developers and engineers. The first step to moving past this hindrance is rebranding yourself as a business owner and continuing to reinvent yourself as needed as your business grows and scales.

Reinventing yourself doesn't mean losing your company's identity, however. Your niche already makes your business unique. It's where you came from and where you're headed, both at the same time. In the next chapter, I'll discuss why niche players always win—and winning battles is what a great army general does!

Key Takeaways

1. The mindset shift from team captain to army general is pivotal.

2. Being the best on the team does not necessarily make you a good leader in business where managing a large team well is essential.

3. Reinventing yourself and operating as a manager, general, or principal (rather than a captain, soldier, or teacher) is necessary for success.

4. Building strong relationships with employees, customers, suppliers, and shareholders is the key responsibility of a business owner.

CHAPTER 10

Why Niche Players Always Win

Millionaire Mentor owned a company that specialized in business intelligence analytics (BI) for large enterprises, particularly large enterprises with SAP back ends. For a long time, the company did not deviate from the niche in the slightest.

Then one day, one of the star employees put a proposal forward to start a mobility business—a business that builds mobile apps that connect back to ERP systems. He wrote up a detailed proposal and presented it to Millionaire Mentor and the other owners in his group in a compelling way.

They found the upcoming mobility market very interesting and exciting, and it looked like a moneymaking opportunity. They approved it and agreed to allocate $100,000 of seed money to get it started. Six months later, the $100,000 was depleted, and they had zero traction. It turned out it was quite hard to sell these projects and that their strong reputation as a BI player held no sway when it came to selling mobility projects.

For Millionaire Mentor's company, there was a stark contrast between the effort required to win a $1 million BI deal vs. the effort required to win a $100,000 mobility deal—it was a lot easier to close the $1 million BI deal. This fact helped them to decide to kill the mobility business. Furthermore, if they wanted to expand, there was an abundance of opportunity within their existing space, such as new regions, open-source big data, more software vendors, BI strategy as a management consulting offer, financial consolidations, and much more.

Steve Jobs once said at Apple's 1997 Worldwide Developers Conference (WWDC), "You've got to say, 'no, no, no,' and when you say 'no,' you piss off people. The smart, good-looking ideas are the ones that take you away from your main priorities."

In another instance, Jobs said, "People think 'focus' means saying yes to the thing you've got to focus on, but that's not what it means at all. It means saying no to the hundred other good ideas that there are. You have to pick carefully. I'm actually as proud of the things we haven't done as the things I have done. Innovation is saying no to a thousand things."[18]

In a tech services business, the temptation to deviate from your core offering is even greater than in a product business. You build great relationships with your customers, and then they ask you, "What else can you guys do for us?" They ask you if you have access to somebody who can do X or somebody who can do Y. And you think to yourself, "This is a real opportunity. This could be the beginning of something big." But, as Steve Jobs attested, the ability to say no, no, no is what separates the men from the mice.

Did Millionaire Mentor and his co-owners give up too quickly on the mobility business? If they kept going with it, could it have succeeded in the long run?

Millionaire Mentor told me he had no doubt that it could have eventually been a huge success! But that's not the right question to ask.

The right question to ask is "What is the opportunity cost? If we'd thrown more time and money at the mobility business, what effect would that have had on the rest of the business?" Could they have done better by spending the time and money on something that fell within their niche? The answer is usually yes. Not only would the new business have a better chance of success, but the rest of the old one would benefit too.

For the purpose of this discussion, I'm defining a niche as a specialty within a specialty. For example, human capital management (HCM) is not a niche, per se. However, Oracle HCM is considered a niche.

Similarly, an industry is not a niche. For example, mining is not a niche; however, production planning for mining companies certainly is a niche. Also, a large software vendor, such as Salesforce, SAP, Oracle, Microsoft, or AWS, cannot be a niche on its own. None of them is a niche specialty, because they're too big. If you have a Salesforce firm, and you ask a Salesforce employee about their brand, what will they say? "Oh yes, that's just another Salesforce shop. We have hundreds of them."

I once met someone who runs a Salesforce firm for nonprofit organizations. Now that is a niche. He employs more than 100 consultants and is growing fast. Salesforce knows exactly when to call them, and they know what to expect. Do they have opportunities for growth? You bet they do. With their offshore offering in place, they can expand into any region they desire. They can also expand into other CRM products. Their specialty in nonprofit is what makes them famous in the Salesforce ecosystem, and this fame can be transferred into other regions and products.

If you're seeking evidence that niche players do better in the tech services space, you don't have to search far. Not only do they get better EBIT multiples when they sell to their bigger counterparts, but they grow faster and have happier employees and, last but not least, happier owners. SPI Research is a professional services research company. They've researched thousands of companies and have concluded that as a rule, the niche players outperform the generalists. Crucially, one of SPI Research's findings is that these top performers spend less money on sales and benefit more from referrals.[19]

Can Generalists Do Well?

For a generalist to do well, it needs to be really large, such as an Accenture or DXC. Such companies consist of practices or divisions, and each is basically a niche business inside a larger one. Ideally, each practice eventually reaches a critical mass. These large firms can create new specialty practices organically, and when they fail at that, they acquire the specialists in trade sale deals.

Their business model clearly works, but only because of the scale. Do not try this on a small scale. To become a generalist on a small scale is a sure way of having a terrible time.

Are Niche Players Too Small?

If we're talking Tier 1, such as Accenture or Deloitte, then yes, niche (as I define it in this book) is probably not on their agenda. But in the Tier 3 space, the niche players will generally outgrow their generalist competitors. Some examples are

- Smart WFM—a specialist human capital management business focused on implementing UKG. They tripled in size in a three-year period. (https://www.consulting.us/news/6859/australian-born-hcm-consultancy-smart-wfm-expands-into-us)

- Plative, Inc—a specialist Salesforce and Oracle implementer for specific target industries. They grew revenue 114 percent from 2021 to 2022. (https://www.consultingmag.com/2022/10/11/the-2022-fastest-growing-firms-plative-inc/)

A niche business can grow to hundreds of consultants and even reach nine-digit revenues before they run out of growth opportunities.

The Three Circles

From the analysis performed by Jim Collins, author of *Good to Great: Why Some Companies Make the Leap and Others Don't*, and his team, it's clear that truly great companies have one thing in common: They know and doggedly stick to their niche. He defines this as the intersection of three circles, also known as "the hedgehog concept":

THE HEDGEHOG CONCEPT - YOUR NICHE

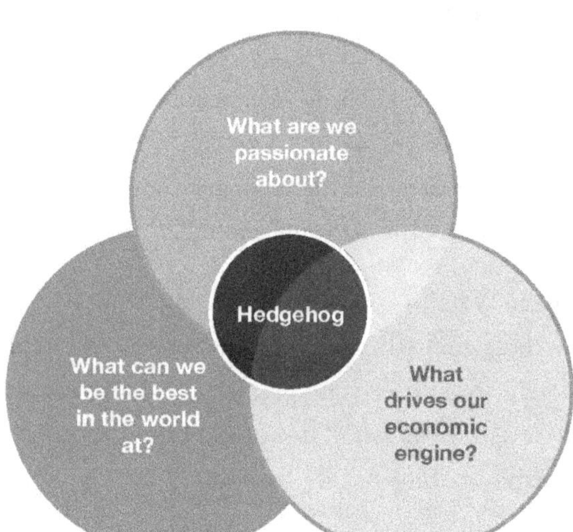

- What are we as a business deeply passionate about?

- In what field can we be the best in the world?

- Do we know the economic drivers for our niche?

Companies he analyzed that were disciplined and rigorous in maintaining their niche consistently outperformed generalist businesses by far.[20]

How Will Saying No Affect the Numbers?

The challenge with a tech services business is that saying yes to everything can help you boost revenue and profit instantly. The gain is short term, but the pain is long term. It's like eating fast food—short-term gain, long-term pain. If, however, you switch gears and say no to work outside your niche, you may have short-term pain, but you'll reap the long-term gain.

When Steve Jobs returned to Apple in 1997, he killed 70 percent of Apple's products. This had an immediate negative impact on revenues, but suddenly, employees knew what to focus on, and one year later, they'd made a whopping $309 million in profit.[21]

The Benefits of Running a Niche Firm

The temptation to diversify is often very appealing. However, once you fully understand all the benefits of a strong niche, it becomes easier to say no. Some benefits of operating within a niche are:

- Reputation as the best in your niche

- Confidence in selling yourself

- Attracting and retaining the best employees in the business

- Lower costs of selling due to a good reputation and high confidence in your offering

- Better EBIT multiples when your specialty solves a potential client's problem

- Better sales funnel

- Fewer escalations because your employees know what they are doing

- Higher profit since you are twice as effective as your competition

- Access to larger accounts (and freedom to say no to smaller accounts)

- Effective marketing frequency

- Brand permission as a result of advocacy from your existing happy clients

- A healthier bench where top-performing consultants can work on new deals, methodologies, marketing materials, etc.

What If My Niche Is Dying?

So, what happens if the niche you chose is not big enough or is dying?

Nothing is permanent. You always have to be on the move. The best way to avoid becoming a victim of a dying industry is to reinvent yourself regularly, as we discussed in the previous chapter, but on a larger scale. If your chosen niche is becoming too small, or if it's dying, then start a new practice that deviates a little but not too much.

At Bluleader, we focused on SAP customer experience, which included things like CRM and commerce. However, SAP CRM just never took off sufficiently, and we became concerned. We noticed that Microsoft CRM was making headway, so we launched an MS CRM practice. This was a deviation from our niche but not a big one.

Making the Leap

So, how do you make the leap and narrow your focus? Not everyone has the confidence of Steve Jobs to cut 70 percent of a company's products instantly. However, that 70 percent did not pertain to *his* products. He had not launched those products, and he had not hired those people. So, killing them was easy for him to do. But what if you're the one who has driven the diversification in your business and now you want to reverse it? You don't want to kill your own babies.

My recommendation is to follow these guidelines:

- Spend zero dollars on marketing for anything that sits outside the niche.

- Double down on marketing and thought leadership for the niche offerings.

- Pay little or zero sales commission on deals outside the niche and pay extra for deals inside the niche.

- Report the numbers separately (core vs. noncore) and track progress over time.

- The company website should not mention your diversified offerings, only your core offerings.

- The leadership team should not spend more than 10 percent of their time on anything outside the niche.

- Be honest with the staff who work in those noncore practices. Tell them they're still important, but the company is building a reputation to be strong in one specific area. They could still benefit indirectly, since this newfound focus will give the business a foot in the door with more customers. Some employees might then choose to make a career change into this niche.

If you decide to narrow your focus, those parts of the business that are not your core will either fade away slowly or become self-sufficient. If they survive and become self-sufficient, then that is a great outcome, since it makes money, takes up little of your time, and does not dilute your marketing message.

A good example of narrowing focus is Duncan Journee, who grew his Microsoft business from $900,000 to $12 million in five years. He grew at 60 percent year over year, and he did this by narrowing down his niche. He started by buying into a business owned by four technical people. He eventually bought them out, but he realized that from day one, he had to pick a niche.

"The first thing I did was interesting because, you see, we did SharePoint, we did Dynamics CRM, and we did a bit of application development," he explained to me on my podcast. "Three things, because they were techies, four technical people. So, the first thing I did was, the quick win, change the website. Secondly, I got a marketing company involved. Then, I said, 'We need to focus. We need to do something. We need to focus on something.'

"So, this is a great story. We had three customers: one in insurance, one in health, and one in associations. Literally, we had equal references in all three of these. I asked the guys, 'What do we know most?' They said, 'Well, we built systems for all three of them.' So, literally, I took a dart, had these three companies on the wall, and I threw it. 'Oh, okay. It's associations!'

"Looking back at that, it's the best thing we did… My philosophy is that you need to differentiate and to stand out. In the world of

Microsoft, there are lots of partners. In fact, there are lots and lots of partners."[22]

There you go, once again demonstrating how powerful a niche can be. If you listen to Journee, you could argue that the exact niche you pick and the decision you make about which one is maybe less important than just deciding. The magic, then, is in sticking to it and focusing all your efforts on that one thing. Incredibly powerful!

So, now you're at the helm of your business, leading as a general (and not a captain), and have selected a solid niche to establish dominance in your field. There's one piece left to this puzzle, and it must be placed precisely. You'll receive that final piece in the next chapter, and then you're well on your way to the strategic portion of growing and scaling your business.

Key Takeaways

1. Always consider opportunity cost when taking on new offerings.

2. Niche players outperform generalists.

3. Your niche is what you should promote. You can still provide other offerings, but they must be executed opportunistically and without distracting from the core business.

CHAPTER 11

Cash Is King, Culture Is Emperor

Bono famously said, "We thought that we had the answers. It was the questions we had wrong."[23]

Some questions in business are small, e.g., "How can we make our website look better?" Alternatively, some questions are big. The big questions are the hardest to answer because they have the biggest impact on the business and on people's lives.

Go study any billionaire and you'll find that they ask big questions.

So, what should be your biggest question? You might argue, "What's our purpose in the world?" is the biggest question, and maybe you're right. If you don't know what your purpose is, then this is certainly the place to start.

However, if your purpose is clear, you are ready to move on to the mother of all questions:

"What is culture?"

Millionaire Mentor shared a story with me that I'd like to relay to you. At his company, they were trying to wrap their heads around culture. They knew culture was important, and they always made an effort to create a good working environment. But as an entrepreneur, you sometimes wonder, "Are we running a business or a charity?"

However, things became clearer on one particular day.

One of the partners attended a networking event where he met with a billionaire businessman. He worked his way through the crowd to get a chance to speak to him. He then asked the billionaire what his secret was in business. The answer came back: "Culture."

As ambitious entrepreneurs, the ownership group at Millionaire Mentor's company suddenly made a new connection in their minds. They realized that culture is not some socialistic idea promoted by HR professionals. Culture is an unstoppable force, and it prints money as a side effect.

It turns out this billionaire is not the only one who believes that culture is the key to financial success. They all believe it. Some of them only realize it in retrospect, but they all reach the same conclusion eventually.

And since that day, the biggest, most important question Millionaire Mentor and his co-owners ever asked themselves was "What is culture?"

So, what *is* it? Well, I can't give you a short answer because there isn't one. Remember, the big questions are hardest to answer. Ask yourself the question regularly, answer it well, and you will succeed in a big way.

How to Create a Bad Culture

A good starting point for any culture enthusiast is to first understand how you can quickly create a bad culture in your business. Unfortunately, this is really easy to do and comes quite naturally.

Here are some tips on how to create a bad culture:

1. Talk poorly about people behind their backs, including your business partners.

2. When your staff talk poorly about others behind their backs, join the conversation.

3. Send out regular emails to all staff and complain about something, such as timesheets being late or anything that bothers you. Encourage your back-office team to do the same.

4. Run a staff update session where you set the agenda and you do all the talking.

5. Tell people what to do, and don't ask them what they think. If you do ask them, they'll think you're incompetent.

6. If one employee abuses a privilege, put some measures in place that apply to everyone, e.g., create a new HR policy and send out an email to everyone to announce it.

7. Fill your vacancies as fast as you can.

8. When you interview potential employees, trust your gut instinct. If you have a good feeling about them, hire them. Do not second-guess yourself.

9. When you hire people, let the recruitment agent do the reference check. That is their specialty. You don't need the reference check anyway since your gut feeling about the candidate is good.

10. Don't fire underperforming employees—that is too cruel.

11. If an employee does not fit in, talk about this person behind their back, but do not fire them.

12. Avoid performance management—too much negative energy.

13. Don't share bad news with staff.

14. If you really have to fire somebody, walk them out the door in front of everyone. But don't do it yourself; that will damage your reputation. Let somebody else do it.

15. If somebody resigns, tell them they're making a big mistake and they will regret it.

16. If a staff member acts out of line, put them back in their place in front of everyone.

17. Tell your employees about the company's plan of action and then don't carry it out.

This is not a complete list by any means. The list is infinite. Just continue to focus on your own desires and feelings and you will succeed in creating a bad culture.

Wow, that was draining. Let's get back into positive-thinking mode.

How to Create a Great Culture

There are many books written on culture, so I will not give you an exhaustive set of answers, but here are some recommendations that will help you on your quest:

1. Run a successful business by applying every strategy in this book.

2. Don't stop at the little culture boosters (Ping-Pong table, free food, benefits, perks). Be intentional and encourage your staff. Give them your full support by helping them achieve their career goals and, in some cases, their personal goals.

3. Define your DNA (the business's core values), and hire those aligned with said core values. Fire the misfits, promote your values relentlessly, and live them every day.

4. Think deeper than money; give your staff a purpose and talk about it regularly.

5. Create excitement about the future by defining an exciting mission, vision, or Big Hairy Audacious Goal (BHAG), and promote those things repeatedly.

6. Be authentic about your values—ones that are already true in the eyes of your customers and staff.

7. Be realistic about the future. (Believe in stretch goals.)

8. Know your type of culture, and stick to it. (Not all companies think alike; don't try to be every type of culture.)

9. Let toxic people go. (What you tolerate becomes your culture.)

10. Lead by example with a healthy mental state because a poor mental state gets tripped up by its own deficient inner workings.

11. Embrace all of the above, and do it right. Take this seriously, and constantly try new initiatives, receive feedback, tweak, and repeat. Find out what works, be intentional, and most importantly, never let up!

Now, if your culture is already bad or nonexistent, there are things you can do to fix it.

Let's look at toxicity in your workplace. Toxic employees are those who do not align with your core values. There's a concept about employees fitting into certain buckets, such as "dogs," "team players," and "brilliant jerks"—the latter is a term coined by Arianna Huffington.[24]

David Shein covers this in his book, *The Dumbest Guy at the Table*, and the message is simple: even if you have brilliant employees, if some of them are outright jerks (and toxic to your culture), you have to help them change their attitudes or transition them out.

Brilliant jerks are not exclusive to employees. Even business owners (your partners) can be brilliant jerks, as in the case of Uber. In that situation, the best move to push the business forward was to get rid of the CEO, which Uber's investors did in 2017.[25]

It all began when former Uber CEO Travis Kalanick announced he was joining former President Donald Trump's advisory board in late 2016. What followed was a storm of protests in San Francisco. His company was then charged with a $20 million fine for recruiting drivers while exaggerating earnings potential. Just one month later, a former Uber engineer posted a blog that chronicled the company's culture of sexism. And days after that, Waymo filed a lawsuit against Uber, alleging the company stole secrets related to autonomous vehicle technology. To top it off, Kalanick was then caught on film yelling at an Uber driver.[26]

There's more to this story of Kalanick's tragic fall from grace. However, this example just goes to show that someone could be so brilliant as to build a company that changes the way the world operates and yet still make things very difficult for fellow shareholders and employees alike.

Another way to fix culture is for company leadership to be authentic—by which I mean brutally honest. Shein told me a story about a situation in which he was consulting with a business whose original owners didn't want him to be honest with their staff about how bad things were at the company. Initially, Shein followed those wishes, but he was eventually grilled by the staff. "How can you say the company is doing well when you just fired the CEO and CFO?"

After the meeting, Shein went to the person assisting him with the presentations and said, "You've been to my house, right? You think I got a house like that by letting people tell me what to put in my presentations? Next time, I'm going to present the truth."

This level of authenticity garners respect from all involved. Be truthful, be authentic, and be a partner to your staff. It will pay dividends in the long run.

Finally, to fix culture, you must remember: you can have the best strategy in the world, but if you have a bad culture, it's all for naught. When Microsoft had a change in leadership a few years back, the company decided it was going to change its mission statement as well. It updated the mission statement to read: "To empower every person and every organization on the planet to achieve more."[27]

Value shifts are important when they are necessary. Embodying those values with intensity and consistency is essential.

In conclusion, the mindset shifts discussed in this section are not the be-all and end-all to your company's success. However, when you use them to build a foundation for the leadership of your organization, you will start the race a quarter of the way ahead of your competition.

In the next section, we will be brutally honest with ourselves in order to assess our Active, or current, State. This will be the driving force in determining the next steps in growing your business. I'll take you from where you are now to your destination goals. To do that, a self-assessment is critical, and that's where we will begin.

Key Takeaways

1. The biggest question for entrepreneurs who already know their purpose is "What is culture?"

2. Culture is an unstoppable force that is key to financial success.

3. To create a great culture, apply strategies from successful business books, support and encourage staff, define your core values, give staff a purpose, lay out an exciting future, and lead by example.

PART III

ACTIVE AND TARGET STATES

CHAPTER 12

Assess Your Active State

American researcher, speaker, and consultant Jim Collins, author of *Good to Great*, tells a story of a conversation he had with Admiral Jim Stockdale, the highest-ranking military officer ever held captive at the infamous Hanoi Hilton prison camp. He was shot down in the 1960s and spent eight years in the camp. Collins had the privilege of speaking with and learning from Stockdale after reading his book *In Love and War: The Story of a Family's Ordeal and Sacrifice During the Vietnam Years*. In the book, Stockdale recounted the bleak experience of his imprisonment.

When asked how on earth he dealt with that level of suffering, Stockdale replied that he never wavered in his faith that not only would he get out, but he would also turn it into the defining moment of his life. He said that, in retrospect, he would not trade.

In awe, Collins followed up, asking Stockdale who didn't make it out as strong as him.

"Oh, that's easy, the optimists," Stockdale said. "Oh, they were the ones who said, 'We're going to be out by Christmas.' And Christmas would come, and Christmas would go. Then they'd say, 'We're going to be out by Easter.' And Easter would come, and Easter would go. And then Thanksgiving, and then it would be Christmas again. And they died of a broken heart."[28]

From this, Collins coined the Stockdale paradox, which is composed of two elements. "This is a very important lesson. You must never confuse faith that you will prevail in the end—which you can never afford to lose—with the discipline to confront the most brutal facts of your current reality, whatever they might be."[29]

Collins noticed that all the leaders of the great companies he researched for *Good to Great* embodied those two elements.

Therefore, to assess your Active State—exactly where you are right now—you must face the brutal facts. You must be ruthless and honest with yourself. Assessing your Active State is not about where you want to be but about looking at the reality of where you are and calling yourself out on it.

This task shouldn't just fall on you, as the owner. No, it should be done with the brain trust within your business. I encourage you to sit down with those key stakeholders, take an objective look at the company, and fill out a comprehensive assessment. Within the assessment, you'll ask yourself what your current perceived competencies are and what your value proposition is. However, crucially, you must approach this from the viewpoint of what's actually being seen out there in the marketplace, not what you hope is being seen.

There are two spaces in which you could live: what you think your value proposition is—your Target State—and what your customers actually perceive—your Active State.

You may say you're the leading BI company in your market and that you ensure all of your analytics are delivered on time to your clients' CFOs. However, the reality could very well be that this is only 5 percent of what your company does, that you're typically late, and that everyone is upset. So, your Active State is what your customers, your suppliers, and your employees are seeing as the truth.

I once worked with a consulting firm that had "supply chain" in its name. They claimed they could administer all forms of SAP. Do you see the fallacy in that? The market's perception, when seeing this company's name, was that the company was a group of supply chain specialists. This is a misalignment in what potential customers see—and expect—and what the company actually does in reality. It's imperative to get your value proposition and the market's perception of you aligned before you can approach the Target State (your ideal company).

Another example could be a disconnect between several teams within your organization. In a services business with 10 customers, all you have to do is talk to the sales team. They'll tell you that they're out there talking to the customers every day and they know what service customers receive on a daily basis. However, the delivery team's perception of the company's strengths could be vastly different. This causes massive tension internally between sales and delivery teams and, ultimately, harms the company. I have seen cases in tech services teams where the sales and delivery teams operate in silos and will try to undermine each other's efforts. The sales team hears from the customer that service levels in support are falling, but the delivery team shows all their quantitative measures as being positive. What they are not reporting is that certain delivery team members have had personality clashes with customer personnel (which sometimes are quite justified), so these team members are working consciously or subconsciously to "lose" the customer.

So, how do you assess your Active State in a brutally honest way? Well, first, you need to gather the brain trust within your company to gain all of those different perspectives. What questions should you ask?

1. Is our mindset where it needs to be? Have we addressed all of the elements from the Mindset portion of the MATE Framework?

2. Are all key shareholders on the same page? Is the relationship healthy?

3. Where does the business really stand? Is each team running like a well-oiled machine? If not, which teams should be improved through better automation and overall performance?

4. Is our niche big enough? Can we grow without horizontal scaling?

5. Is our profit and loss where it needs to be in order to further grow and scale?

6. What are the strengths of our leadership team? What are the strengths of our doers?

Answering these questions may be uncomfortable because the Active State, in a nutshell, is made up of both the good and the bad. However, with the right mindset, you should be able to fairly evaluate the pros and cons of your business's reality.

To complete your assessment, familiarize yourself with the following key terms and concepts. Then define each of these for your situation and use them as your North Star, your guiding force in sticking with your plan to scale.

Big Hairy Audacious Goal (BHAG). The BHAG is a stretch vision for your business. It should be bold enough to be challenging but also realistic enough that it is feasible. Rallying around this BHAG is a powerful way to ensure you are always on track. It's also a pivotal key for success and life balance. Here are some examples of BHAGs:

- *A computer on every desk and in every home*—Microsoft

- *Make humanity multiplanetary*—SpaceX

- *Organize the world's information*—Google

A revenue- or profit-based target BHAG can be exciting for some people, but you need to ensure that it's something your entire team can get behind. With qualitative targets, make sure it's clear to everyone throughout the business how success will be measured. There are four types of BHAGs:

- *Target-based—achieve $100 million revenue within 10 years*

- *Competitive—be the first in the world to offer subscription-based cars*

- *Role model-based—be the Harvard of Southeast Asia*

- *An internal transformation—move all transactions to digital and eliminate bricks and mortar*

Your BHAG can fall within one or a combination of these categories.

Targets (3 to 5 years). Working backward from the BHAG, determine what needs to be achieved within the next three to five years. These goals will be quantitative and should cover revenue, EBIT, and employee numbers, or any other applicable quantitative measures for your business. These targets will provide a road map to the BHAG.

Goals (1 year). Once you've identified the 3- to 5-year goals, define what needs to be achieved within the next year. Again, these goals will be quantitative, covering revenue, EBIT, and employee numbers.

Long-Term Initiatives (3- to 5-year priorities). To achieve the 3- to 5-year numbers, what capabilities or pillars must first be built? These can be things like

- *a sales team of three with an industry best-in-class sales director within five years, or*

- *three fully established practices with revenues of $5 million each.*

Current-Year Initiatives (annual priorities). Looking at the 3-to-5-year priorities, which of these can you tackle within the next year? To plan for each priority, break down the activities needed to get it established. For example, to establish three practices, we need to start with one. To create a practice, the key activities could be four steps:

1. Find and hire a strong practice manager.

2. Find and hire a strong technical lead.

3. Create a go-to market (GTM) for the practice.

4. Win the first deal for the practice.

So when looking at annual priorities, you might decide you need to achieve the first three activities on this list. You would then create one annual priority for this activity called "Establish practice leadership with defined GTM." As always, ensure the goals are achievable but are also stretching enough to move your business forward at the correct pace to reach the BHAG and 3- to 5-year goals.

Core Values and Beliefs. These are the attributes of your best staff that you would like all hires to exhibit. Once articulated, your core values and beliefs should play a large part in defining the culture and vision of the business and be a key tool for recruiting and the ongoing benchmarking of your staff. Employees and/or contractors should not just have the right skills but also embody these values and beliefs.

The important thing to note here is that these values should not be just nebulous, made-up terms posted on a wall in the building or on the "About Us" page of your website. They should be a part of your best people's DNA already.

Author, speaker, and president of management consultant firm The Table Group, Patrick Lencioni, wrote an article about this topic for the *Harvard Business Review*. In summary,

"Core values are the deeply ingrained principles that guide all of a company's actions; they serve as its cultural cornerstones. [Jim] Collins and [Jerry] Porras succinctly define core values as being inherent and sacrosanct; they can never be compromised, either for convenience or short-term economic gain. Core values often

reflect the values of the company's founders—Hewlett-Packard's celebrated 'HP Way' is an example. They are the source of a company's distinctiveness and must be maintained at all costs.

"*Aspirational values* are those that a company needs to succeed in the future but currently lacks. One company I worked with valued extremely hard work and dedication; its employees were known to work late into the evenings and on weekends. At some point, the executive team felt compelled to add 'work/life balance' as an aspirational value, but they ultimately decided against it because it would confuse employees about what mattered most to the company.

"*Permission-to-play values* simply reflect the minimum behavioral and social standards required of any employee.

"*Accidental values* arise spontaneously without being cultivated by leadership and take hold over time. They usually reflect the common interests or personalities of the organization's employees. Accidental values can be good for a company, such as when they create an atmosphere of inclusivity. But they can also be negative forces, foreclosing new opportunities. Managers need to distinguish core values from merely accidental ones, as confusion here can be disastrous."[30]

Therefore, it is critical to evaluate your current staff as well as your new hires against the values you set to determine if you have the right people in place who will embody those core values and beliefs.

Purpose. Your business's purpose should be higher than simply what is delivered day-to-day. It should articulate the greater reason for your business's existence. Examples of purpose include the following:

- To eliminate bad customer service

- To make the lives of every retired person meaningful

- To connect the world

Your purpose needs to be measurable and exciting. Your people should be motivated by their potential to change the world.

Current Perceived Competencies. The key capabilities of the business as perceived by your market and customers.

Current Value Proposition. What your customers can expect to receive as a value or experience every time they engage with you. Consider this your elevator pitch. The more consistently you can deliver on that promise, the greater your value proposition will be with your customers and employees. This needs to be measurable, not vague. Some examples include

- 24-hour delivery within the metro guaranteed, or your money back,

- Lowest prices guaranteed, and

- 99.99% availability without compromise.

Current Market. This element is about defining your niche as a business and should cover both capability and geographical elements. Knowing the market allows you to drive key decisions in the future around expansion. The market should be focused enough to be clear for all but also provide access to a market large enough to meet your targets. These are some example markets:

- Azure cloud migration services across the UK

- Public sector business process automation implementation services within Australia and New Zealand

Strengths, Weaknesses, Opportunities, Threats (SWOT). Understanding your SWOT is a key factor in knowing your Active State. This should be defined within your current context and not where you will be in the future.

Target Perceived Competencies. Once you have identified your Target State, you must understand what competencies are required to reach it and what is needed to obtain these if you do not already have them. These may be the same as they are now, or there may be others.

Target Value Proposition. What will the value proposition (described in Active State elements above) be in your Target State?

Target Market. What will the market (described in Active State elements above) be in your Target State?

In keeping with the theme of being honest with yourself, there is yet another step in assessing your Active State. We've faced the brutal facts, but now we must face the demons. In the next chapter, we'll discuss what things (or people) are potentially damaging your Active State and how to address them so that you can focus on the bigger picture.

Key Takeaways

1. To assess your Active State, you must face the brutal facts and be ruthless and honest with yourself.

2. Assessing your Active State is not about where you want to be but about looking at the reality of where you are and calling yourself out on it.

3. Gather your company's brain trust to gain different perspectives when assessing your Active State in an open and honest way.

CHAPTER 13

Face the Demons

A major part of acknowledging the brutal facts is the difficult yet necessary task of facing your company's demons. But what exactly are those demons?

The most pressing, and what we'll chiefly discuss in this chapter, are individuals who make life more difficult within your organization.

It was a Monday morning when Millionaire Mentor spoke to one of his co-owners, whom we'll call Frank, on the phone to discuss the company's numbers. They had come a long way since being best friends in primary school. At age 12, Frank moved far away, and Millionaire Mentor did not see him again until years later. As adults, they continued their friendship. They bought a small boat together, went sailing on weekends, and eventually became business partners. As friends, they never argued, never fought, never competed, and were never jealous of each other.

The next thing they knew, they were yelling at each other over the phone on that Monday morning. In 30 years of friendship, neither had ever yelled at the other, and they were both surprised and shocked that it happened. People make so many jokes about marriage, but for every joke about marriage, a similar joke can be told about business partnerships.

The good news, though, is that relationships between business partners don't have to be first class. The objective is to be functional, not to become best friends. If you do end up making a new friend in the process, well, consider that a bonus.

During their journey together running that company, the founders had a multitude of coaches and advisors who helped them along their way. One such person was a man we'll call Dennis. The ownership group considered him a real grandfather figure. He taught the founders many things, but the most memorable was that the four founders should be tight. They should not allow anyone to come between them. That was such important advice.

As your business grows and as you start hiring people who are smarter than you, you will inevitably deal with employees whose aim is to divide and conquer. This is the oldest strategy in the book. Every once in a while, they will throw bait—things like "Bob seems to be shying away from sales responsibilities."

Bob is your partner, and although this employee's remark might be true, you cannot take the bait.

The founders discussed Dennis's advice to stay tight and made a pledge that they wouldn't tolerate gossip about each other, and certainly not from their employees. Years later, one of the top employees commented, "You guys seem to be backing each other real hard."

That was reassuring to hear, Millionaire Mentor recounted, and there is no doubt that the decision to present a united front helped his company greatly along the way.

When, inevitably, there are personality clashes, you should be aware of them and zoom in. Starting at the top, ask yourself, "Do our founders (or shareholders) get along with one another? Are we all working toward the same objectives?"

Sometimes, it can come down to getting everyone to agree on an exit strategy and the terms of a deal. In this case, you must home in on what causes conflict between your ownership groups, map out a solution, and write it on a nonbinding piece of paper. By nonbinding, I mean that it's not legally binding. This should be written at the top of the document.

Of course, you may also encounter minor disagreements on processes or plans, but overall, the owners or founders of a company should at least get along. It's not about personalities but objectives.

Another demon—or rather, clash—within your organization could stem from differences in values. Here are the most important steps to take as an ownership group to get everyone on the same page.

Establish and Build Upon Trust

In Patrick Lencioni's book *The Five Dysfunctions of a Team*, he encourages business professionals to figure out why things have become dysfunctional in the first place. He says they typically fall within these five areas:

1. Absence of trust

2. Fear of conflict

3. Lack of commitment

4. Avoidance of accountability

5. Inattention to results

So, make your way to a private room, close the door, and establish first and foremost that you and your ownership group all have each other's backs no matter what so that when you come out, you will no longer have a dysfunctional conflict. A healthy team can have conflict but still achieve great results.

The basis of a healthy team is trust. By this, Lencioni means that the business is a safe environment for people to say, "These are my weaknesses, and I can tell you I have enough trust in the team for others to compensate for those weaknesses." If those weaknesses are used against that person in another forum, that will kill trust. Can people be honest with each other? Can that information stay in the room and not be used later as a weapon?

Recently, I started working with a new client who had decided to leave her current company to start up a new one. On her way out the door, her former boss said to her, "Whoever your partner is, they'd better be good with operations."

Rather than tucking that comment away and allowing it to eat at her, she told her new partner the story. The fact that she was comfortable doing so indicates a deep level of trust between them. She knew there wouldn't be gossip outside her relationship with her new business partner.

So, once you have trust established, you can move on to the next level. Conflict is about thrashing ideas around. If you don't have conflict because people can't speak up (due to lack of trust), no one will be aligned with the decision that gets made by the group.

This, then, leads to a lack of commitment. Perhaps half the room is silently not committing because they don't buy into the decision, since the conflict wasn't brought up in the first place. Without commitment, no one wants to take accountability because they don't back the decision that's being made. What happens? There is no attention to results, and ultimately you don't get outcomes.

So, how do you fix this? You have to address it from the outset. If someone in that room is sitting quietly, you have to challenge them. "Hey, do you agree with what's being said?" Really demand their input. It's the job of the facilitator of this meeting to create "healthy conflict" within that environment of trust. The goal is to flesh out fresh ideas. You don't want people in the room simply agreeing to agree. Do they genuinely agree with what's being discussed? If not, they should feel comfortable in saying what they want/need to say and feel free to engage in healthy debate around their opinions.

Make a Short List of Existing Issues and Resolve Them

Plenty of people never bring up these issues, and if they do, they raise them out of the blue and not in a structured way.

It's not constructive to only bring up conflicts every once in a while. When it comes to a partnership, you need to sit down regularly and make a list of issues with your shareholders—not because you want to point fingers, but because you want to work through them. You have to be proactive, not reactive.

Once you have identified all the areas of conflict within your ownership group, I recommend that you create a nonbinding document that summarizes the issues and proposed resolutions as you work through them. It could be a whiteboard, a mind map, or a word processing document. It is up to you, but the idea is to reach a point of agreement where everyone can move forward and use this nonbinding document as a compass.

Again, it's important that it is not legally binding; otherwise, the discussion will take on a very different tone.

For this exercise, you may want to enlist a facilitator because, depending on the relationships and personalities in the room, it could get messy. An external person can keep everyone calm and composed. This step is not to be taken lightly.

Conflict could be about anything—it's not possible to cover all scenarios—but I'll list out what, in my experience, are the most typical that arise. Read through them, and ignore the ones not relevant in your situation. But be sure to think beyond this list, too, because, as we discussed above, conflict can be about anything.

1. **Money.** Some conflicts are mild, and some are severe. Examples include thinking about money all the time, avoiding thinking about money, thinking money is evil, thinking money is more important than relationships, spending more than you earn, being overly frugal, taking excessive risks, and avoiding risks altogether. Ideally,

the business takes well-measured risks with owners and managers who don't have these disorders, but that idea is not seated in reality. Solve these issues before they create dysfunctional relationships.

2. **Timing.** Most people will go through a phase in their lives when they are willing to sacrifice a lot in order to make money. But you might be unfortunate in catching your partner at the wrong phase of their life. For each of us, our hunger for success changes regularly as we move between life phases.

3. **Values.** Relationship issues between partners often come down to conflicting values, such as keeping secrets, unscrupulous business practices, and general moral/religious beliefs. These can be because

   a. one partner is solely focused on making money, while another is solely focused on positive social impacts.

   b. one partner is comfortable with blurring the ethical lines when it comes to taxation or compliance, but the others are not.

   c. one partner believes in an extremely authoritarian leadership style, while the other has a more democratic approach.

   While value clashing is somewhat avoidable by simply picking a compatible partner in the first place, many value conflicts will only be discovered down the track when it's too late to pull out.

4. **Status.** If partners have equal shareholding, then equal

status is certainly most desirable. The most wonderful example is the founders of Google, Sergey Brin and Larry Page, who were 50/50 every step of the way. Somehow, one never developed a desire to stand out above his partner. But this is an unlikely outcome for most—it really is the exception to the rule. And furthermore, if there are more than two partners, it becomes very impractical. For most companies, there comes a time in its growth when it needs to appoint a leader. And when that leader owns a similar number of shares to his/her co-owners, you might be facing some problems, such as undermining practices, ego, and general confusion at board meetings.

All these issues—and more—must be addressed to achieve a synergetic relationship with your business partners. Taking the above steps to mitigate them is a key component in facing your demons.

Design Lifestyles for Each Other

As a business matures, partners will naturally start thinking about their lifestyles. In the early days, the business itself is likely the lifestyle. The privilege to work hard in a new business that will become successful might be the ideal lifestyle for some. But as time goes on and as the novelty diminishes, partners will start resenting their lifestyle compromises—the lack of family vacations, working on weekends, giving up sports, hobbies, time with family and friends, etc.

Having an exit strategy in place, however, can reduce levels of resentment. The future exit becomes the light at the end of the tunnel that makes everything worthwhile.

When partners disagree about work-life balance, the tension it causes risks paralyzing relationships. One partner might believe that everyone should put their personal lives on hold, and another might feel that their nine-to-five commitment is more than sufficient. One partner might argue that the original purpose of the business was to provide better lifestyles for the partners, while another might contend that the better lifestyle will happen in the future, not now.

So, what's the solution?

Partners should genuinely care about each other's lifestyles and look for opportunities to help each other out.

Millionaire Mentor and I had numerous discussions on this topic when I was with Bluleader. On one occasion, I quickly identified some resentments I had been internalizing.

- I was not able to switch off in the evenings when I spent time with my family.

- I never took vacations.

- I never traveled anymore. (I love traveling.)

- I had stopped playing my Gibson Les Paul guitar.

We agreed that I would:

- Aim to work normal hours.

- Switch off my phone in the evenings.

- Start booking vacations.

- Take at least one business trip per year to attend a global conference, and my wife should go with me if possible.

- Start playing guitar again.

Booking my first vacation was hard for me. I just could not get myself to do it—it was almost as if I had forgotten how. It took me months to make my first booking. But when I returned from my first trip, I was invigorated. Millionaire Mentor asked me if I already had my next vacation in mind. I did indeed, so I went ahead and booked it. As a matter of fact, from that point on, I always had my next vacation booked, and I still do today.

Time away made me better at my job. I always came back with tons of energy, and those vacations gave my staff the opportunity to step up within the company and take on more responsibility. I stopped answering phone calls in the evenings, and I really started enjoying my weekends. Finally, I was able to relax without guilt.

As for the guitar, I did not get back into it for a little while, but eventually I did. If you ask me now, I'd say vacations and freeing up my weekends were my biggest breakthroughs.

So, what should you and your partner(s) do to address the work-lifestyle balance? Here are three steps to follow:

1. Have the lifestyle discussion by booking a two- to four-hour meeting and allowing each member of the group to share their ideal post-exit lifestyle. Then, move on to pre-exit lifestyles. Write down everything. There is no need to make decisions; however, you must acknowledge one another's dreams and not devalue them.

2. Reach out to each other after a few weeks by setting a follow-up meeting (also a decision-free meeting) to see where people stand and how their thoughts have progressed.

3. Set a final meeting where you document everything. In

this meeting, go ahead and make life-changing decisions that will make people happy.

Have an A3 Strategy

I will go into an A3 Strategy in more detail in the Execution section of this book. I'm simply noting it here as a key element to achieving mutual agreement among shareholders.

For now, keep in mind that this is more than just a piece of paper. It's a strong technique that will create alignment. Everyone will gather around it and give their input, and it will potentially flush away a lot of conflict. An A3 Strategy can potentially kill off all the demons identified in this chapter.

One of the things that ruins relationships, personal or in business, is when people have different ideas about where the business is going. If you have a group of people, and half of them think they're climbing one mountain while the other half think they're climbing another, it's going to be difficult to move forward. The discussion will be easier when everyone is in alignment on what mountain they're about to climb.

As a business owner, you might assume everyone is climbing the same mountain. Having an exit plan everyone agrees on takes care of the *what*. But you also have to think about the *how*, and this is where disagreements can arise.

Everything you lay out in the A3 Strategy helps you resolve that conflict.

If you don't have this one-page strategy, there's going to be serious misalignment. You'll pull in different directions. You'll sabotage each other's efforts. And you'll do this because you believe this is how you're going to get to the top of the mountain, while another person says they're going to go around the back. Better to put yourself in a situation where you're supporting rather than sabotaging each other.

Keep a Risk Register

Things will go wrong from time to time. Sometimes, things will go terribly wrong. But there is no need to live in fear because fear will ruin the relationships between partners. Fear will paralyze you, and it will paralyze the business.

No two people are equally risk averse. There will always be one person who has no sense of risk and another who is highly risk averse. These differences can cause conflict and become one of your major demons.

The question is "How does one overcome such a demon?"

To tackle and overcome fear, start by creating a risk register in a spreadsheet, and write down all the things that could go wrong. Don't do this just before going into a sales meeting because the discussion will make you depressed. However, it's important to have the discussion.

Go through this spreadsheet once a year so that everyone gets a chance to have their say.

For each risk, write down the mitigation (how to reduce the chance of it happening) and the reaction (what you will do when it happens).

The first item on the list should be "A major fallout between partners." The mitigation might be to implement everything in this chapter, and the reaction might be to engage a mediator. You might even decide to appoint the person in advance.

The second item on the list might be "Major revenue loss." The mitigation might be to prioritize a healthier revenue spread across customers, and the reaction might be to scale down the business and pay out redundancies.

One of the partners might not like the idea of firing staff and object to this strategy. But the point is (and it's an important one): *you want to face the conflict and have these discussions before the tragedy happens.*

If these debates happen in the middle of the tragedy, relationships could be scarred indefinitely. However, if it was agreed up front that the business will trim down, then the pain will be reduced.

Study One Another

There is no silver bullet for chemistry. It's just one of those things that happens between people, or it does not. However, it is possible to improve chemistry, and it is certainly possible to reduce irritation, aggravation, and many other negative emotions that tend to creep into relationships.

Basically, it comes down to personality types. My best advice is to get personality profiling done on all partners. The most popular personality profiling tools are Myers–Briggs (or MBTI) and DISC. Online tools are available; however, I strongly recommend that you get this carried out professionally.

There are a lot of books and materials out there on personality tests. We won't spend time on these, but there is value to them. We recommend billionaire hedge fund owner Ray Dalio's PrinciplesYou at principlesyou.com. Dalio and organizational psychologist Dr. Adam Grant developed this to "help you gain the self-awareness and other-awareness that are critical to making good decisions and getting things done."[31]

Personality assessments will help your leadership better allocate roles within the organization to drive individuals' strengths and improve upon weaknesses, as well as creating a more cohesive and collaborative culture. This is particularly beneficial if you have many smaller teams that work very closely together.

You may receive some initial opposition from your co-founders in understanding the personalities within your organization. From my own experience, I've discovered that founders shy away from personality assessments because they may expose false beliefs held by other founders or CEOs that they are not suited to be founders and CEOs. The fact of the matter is that when you go out and find successful people, they will encompass many different personality types. That's the reason they have been successful in their careers—because they were surrounded by complementary personality types.

For example, Dalio says, "A creative person who is unreliable might be matched with someone who is reliable but not creative. Knowing what people are like also allows us to decide what responsibilities to give them and to weigh our decision with people's merits."[32]

Further, if you don't understand a co-founder's or an employee's personality, you may mistake this lack of connection as a weakness, which can blind you to that individual's strengths. With this approach, rather than saying, "John needs to work with Amy because John is a big thinker who lacks organization skills, and Amy is a meticulous project manager," you'll say, "John thinks too abstractly and can't stay on track with his projects. Let's fire John." Now, you leave Amy on an island, because Amy is a doer, not a thinker. What results is a project that hits every milestone on time but lacks vision and innovation.

Entrepreneurs want to hire jacks-of-all-trades—people who can do everything. However, in a tech services business, that type of corner cutting is dangerous. If everyone you hired were perfect, and they had every skill, they would've started their own companies. The reason they didn't is that they have weaknesses and want to be a part of a team so that others can fill in their gaps and offer support where they need it.

Once you create a culture where most people openly talk about their strengths and weaknesses, then they can help each other out.

Evaluate the Toxic People

On the flip side, just because you've evaluated personalities and worked on getting the best out of all of your teams, there may still be pockets of trouble within those teams.

Further down the line, you might find yourself with a few bad apples, otherwise known as toxic people. These individuals may be some of the smartest in the room, but if they're constantly dragging the organization down with their complaining or a lack of vision toward the bigger picture, then they will be a detriment.

The longer you wait to address these issues, the bigger the problem becomes.

A personality-profiling tool will not fix issues surrounding toxic people. There will still be that 10 to 20 percent where no number of Myers–Briggs tests, personality assessments, or discussions about supporting one another will make a difference. You have to figure out how to either neutralize these individuals (breathe new life into them) or get rid of them.

To make breakthroughs with these demons, you have to first understand yourself and your situation. You have to leave your ego at the door because, in most cases, these clashes are not rooted in someone's distaste for you or another, nor does this mean that anyone's trying to undermine you. These toxic individuals likely have some form of personality disorder. They could be narcissists, psychopaths, or sociopaths. These people exhibit extremely self-centered views, or delusions of grandeur, and can be psychologically abusive and dishonest.

Narcissists are a sliding scale. You can work with borderline narcissists, which can actually be beneficial to your business, because they are typically high performers. But it will be very unpleasant. The trick here is to simply know how to identify them, because narcissists can be wolves in sheep's clothing—very charming at first, but the red flags will eventually begin to pop up.

You should also be careful not to just label someone as having a personality disorder because you plain just don't like them. If you believe someone has a personality disorder, and you tell yourself you can't work with them, go and check the facts by doing a quick assessment online. One question that pops up might be "Does the person apologize for his actions?" If the answer is yes, you are likely not dealing with a full-fledged narcissist but just someone on the border. You can work with that, if you're up for the challenge, by changing *your* attitude and how *you* react to things.

However, if that person is important or powerful enough and is really causing you severe migraines on a regular basis, you may want to aim for an exit and simply get out, and then promise yourself you'll never work with a narcissist again.

Have an Exit Plan

So, whatever happened to Frank and Millionaire Mentor? They did not yell at each other again, but the tension continued to grow in a passive-aggressive way. In fact, the tension among all four of the founders grew, until one day when they had their first breakthrough. They agreed on an exit plan.

It was like the exit plan breathed life into their relationships. "Let's grow this thing hard, then sell it hard, so that we never have to talk to each other again," Frank said jokingly. The reality is they all still stay in touch today and even go on vacations together. But at the time, they needed a break from each other, and the exit plan gave them a channel.

Write down your exit plan. Write down your goal sales price and how long it will take you to get there. Keep reminding each other about that exit.

Now that we've addressed the personalities—both within your ownership group and your employee base—the exciting time has come to map out your ideal company. In the next chapter, we'll talk about the ultimate goal—that most important, larger-than-life dream that gets you to the exit and provides you with the life you always wanted when you first set out to start your business!

Key Takeaways

1. You must face the brutal facts of a company, which includes identifying individuals who make life more difficult.

2. Business partnerships do not need to be first class but should be functional, and gossip should not be tolerated between business partners.

3. Personality clashes can arise in a company, and owners/founders should ensure that they get along with each other.

4. To address dysfunctional issues, owners should establish trust within their ownership group by creating a safe environment for open communication.

5. Conflict within a team is healthy if there is established trust and a safe platform that allows for thrashing ideas around to align on decisions made.

CHAPTER 14

Your Ideal Company

The last two chapters were heavy stuff, weren't they? Yes, facing the brutal facts and coming head-to-head with your demons is tough work, but it has been necessary to get you to this point. Now for the fun part! Let's discuss shaping your vision for your ideal company.

Above all else, if you take nothing else way from this section, know that the most important element in crafting this vision is your Big Hairy Audacious Goal—your BHAG.

First coined by Jim Collins and Jerry Porras in their book, *Built to Last: Successful Habits of Visionary Companies*, the BHAG has become a staple and an inspiration to thousands of companies since its inception in the mid-1990s.[33]

"A BHAG is clear and compelling, needing little explanation; people get it right away," Collins says on his website. "Think of the NASA moon mission of the 1960s. The best BHAGs require both building for the long term AND exuding a relentless sense of urgency: What do we need to do today, with monomaniacal focus, and tomorrow, and the next day to defy the probabilities and ultimately achieve our BHAG?"[34]

Your BHAG is no small feat. At first, it may be something others scoff at, but as you make strides toward your vision, they will be nodding their heads in approval. When you get there, you can say, "See? It was a lofty goal, but it was possible, and we did it!"

"We're talking about a challenge that is so audacious, outside-the-box, and hairy that it might feel as if you'd never achieve it," said Verne Harnish, the founder of the Entrepreneurs' Organization and author of *Scaling Up*. "We're talking about a 'put a man on the moon' level goal here. However, your BHAG **must be connected to your company's underlying strategy** or else, it just becomes an aspirational statement or a random number."[35]

We discussed the BHAG briefly in chapter 12. Again, it is your North Star. If you divert from your path to the exit, then you must look up at your BHAG and remember why you are here and where you are headed. Without it, you'll stay small, and you don't want that. Your BHAG prevents you from thinking small. Thinking small is for your short-term goals. Those short-term goals are important, but they only exist because you have a solid BHAG.

So, to arrive at your target, you will need to create a picture in your mind of what you want your company to look like when it has reached its ideal state—an exercise that you and your co-owners should do and revisit regularly. As discussed already throughout this book, this is your ultimate dream. Once you identify it, the next step is to break it down into parts. You will use this visualization when times are tough to remind yourself and the team why you are on your chosen path. You will also use it when setting short-term goals to ensure they stay in line with the dream.

As you are formulating your vision of your ideal company, ask yourselves these types of detailed questions:

1. What will our customers look and behave like?

2. How many people will we have employed?

3. How many direct reports will we have?

4. What kind of financials will we have, i.e., revenue, profit, and dividends?

5. What will our workdays and weeks look like?

6. How many vacations will we each have per year?

7. How will our business be impacting the world positively?

8. What will our company culture be?

We've discussed many of these factors already. Now it's time to map them out. Once you have answered these questions and visualized what ideal looks like for you, write it all down. If you have a team, use a Post-it Note exercise to brainstorm people's ideas as they occur.

When a concrete ideal has been formulated, you can start to work backward from that ideal to a set of 5-year goals, 1-year goals, and quarterly anchors. Breaking down a goal is a powerful way of inspiring you as you realize that the dream is not as unattainable as it seems when looked at in isolation. For example, if your current business revenue is $1 million, and your ideal is a $10 million business, then you can break it down as follows (do this exercise on a whiteboard):

THE 5-YEAR BREAKDOWN

Year	Revenue Target	Qty. of Employees Producing Revenue	Qty. of Customers	Growth Rate%
5	$10 million revenue	40 employees needed, i.e., hire 2.25 new employees per quarter	Grow current customer revenue by 15% = $9 million 4 new customers at $250,000 each	28% (From this point, a 25% growth rate is achievable and sustainable.)
4	$7.8 million revenue	31 employees needed, i.e., hire 1.5 new employees per quarter	Grow current customer revenue by 20% = $7.2 million 4 new customers at $200,000 each	30% (A sustainable rate for a growth business.)
3	$6 million revenue	24 employees needed, i.e., hire 2 new employees per quarter	Grow current customer revenue by 25% = $5 million 4 new customers at $250,000 each	50% (Rate will slow at this point but is still healthy.)

Year	Revenue Target	Qty. of Employees Producing Revenue	Qty. of Customers	Growth Rate%
2	$4 million revenue	16 employees needed, i.e., hire 2 new employees per quarter	Grow current customer revenue by 50% = $3 million 4 new customers at $250,000 each	100%
1	$2 million revenue	8 employees needed, i.e., hire 1 new employee per quarter	Grow current customer revenue by 50% = $1.5 million 2 new customers at $250,000 each	100% (Very achievable when you are at this size.)
0 (present)	$1 million	4 employees producing $250,000 per annum each	3 customers at $330,000 per annum each	

Once you have set these annual goals, break them down into quarterly priorities, which we will discuss later. Focusing on well-defined quarterly goals will incrementally get you to your ideal company and is a key part of the A3 Strategy covered in the Execution section of this book.

You are now ready to really dive deep into assessing where you are regarding how your business operates. We've discussed being brutally honest about your business's Active State, facing the demons within the business, and what your vision for your ideal company might look like. The next and final step, before taking action, is to evaluate the operation—the engines that keep the business running day-to-day.

In the next chapter, you'll learn about the eight "always-on" engines that, when set up properly, will allow you to step away from being in the weeds and toward being able to grow toward achieving your exit strategy.

Key Takeaways

1. Crafting the vision for your ideal company requires a Big Hairy Audacious Goal (BHAG), which is clear, compelling, and connected to your company's underlying strategy.

2. Your BHAG is your North Star, which prevents you from thinking small and helps you to stay focused on your long-term goals.

3. To arrive at your goal, create a picture in your mind of what you would like your company to look like when it has reached its Target State, and break it down into parts.

CHAPTER 15

Introducing the Eight "Always-On" Engines

The eight "always-on" engines within a business are designed to create growth and progress on an ongoing basis. These key engines should be "always on" or automated and never slowed down by another engine. When you get this right, your business will grow in a scalable way with less and less involvement from you as an owner. To further simplify your business strategy, I've broken the engines down into three distinct categories. Below I'll show you the ideal picture of how each engine should operate.

Once you've read this information, you should rate your business's Active State numerically across various areas within each of the engines. I'll give you some baseline questions to ask yourself.

However, if you're looking for an out-of-the-box way to assess each of these areas, I recommend taking my online assessment at sweat2scale.com.

THE 8 TECH SERVICES ENGINES

The Winning Work Engines

The Demand Engine

This engine is all about constantly putting your organization out to the world as a leader in its field, the first one that customers call upon when help is needed in their niche. The key is to elevate the company so it's perceived as larger and better than it looks on paper, not by lying but through thought leadership.

Within a technology services business, an "always-on" demand-generation engine is critical for creating a constant stream of business. For many businesses in the start-up phase, this engine is ignored in favor of dependency on word-of-mouth promotion. Demand-generation marketing sits just above the sales and marketing funnel, helping attract your target market into becoming aware of your brand and business. Without demand generation, you will struggle to create broad awareness of your company or your offerings, meaning limited visibility to your broader target market.

Demand-generation marketing will help your business by:

- Increasing brand awareness—getting more people interested in your brand and offerings

- Generating more leads—converting more people into prospective customers

- Growing revenue and profits

- Improving lead quality and volume

The typical demand-generation activities that work well for a technology services business are:

- Blog posts

- Webinars

- Videos

- Downloadable content

- Podcasts

- Search Engine Optimization

- Influencer marketing

- Face-to-face events with client speakers, e.g., breakfast events

A few techniques for increasing brand awareness:

- **Define your brand identity.** This entails developing a brand that resonates with the audience you'd like to attract. Your values, purpose, mission statements, work culture, and the visual components of your website are all part of your brand identity.

- **Identify buyer personas/target audience.** Understand your target persona, what their pain point is, and what solutions they're looking for, and detail as much as you can about them. Encapsulate this information into one person—that's your first buyer persona. As you gain new knowledge, keep adding to this persona to stay in sync with your customers.

- **Demonstrate your expertise.** Also known as "thought leadership," this is the expression of proof that you have experience in your industry. It creates a sense of authority, allowing your target market to recall your brand through demand-generation efforts.

- **Have a robust social media presence.** As social media is such a large component of our lives, for your brand to be known, your company must have an active presence on social sites. Users spend an average of 2.5 hours on social media every day, so you need to get out there and make a strong impact.

- **Create a demand-generation strategy.** Put all the research you've done, all the groundwork, and convert it into an executable strategy. Take action and then refine it until you see the numbers you require to get your business to where you want it to be.

When assessing this part of your business, ask yourself where you stand on all of the above. You may want to include some of these questions:

1. Do you proactively generate demand via content creation, e.g., blogs, webinars, and podcasts?

2. Is there an alignment between how you define your brand identity and what your target market and business community know about you?

3. To what extent do you control the community within your niche, or at least stand out in someone else's community?

4. Do you currently measure customer satisfaction?

5. Do you have a robust process for client referrals?

The Lead Engine

This engine is about generating leads that are nurtured and progress efficiently via a sales process that provides a great customer experience.

Lead generation is converting your target audience into qualified leads—people who might want to purchase from you—through a process called "lead scoring."

Lead scoring is the method of quantifying the quality of that potential customer. It draws from the pool created by demand generation and determines their willingness to become paying customers.

Examples of lead sources include:

- Retargeting campaigns

- Whitepapers

- Direct mail marketing

- eBooks

- Live events

How Demand Generation and Lead Generation Work Together

There is some overlap between demand generation and lead generation, which is why people can sometimes use them interchangeably, but these two concepts are very different things. The key difference is that demand generation is a long-term play while lead generation is a short-term play.

Critically, you must ensure you have an "always-on" engine performing both sets of activities.

Demand generation builds company, product, or brand awareness with your target market. It gets your company known, which is how lead-generation campaigns capitalize. There needs to be an awareness of your solutions before there can be interest in buying.

Not everyone who comes to your website or social media feeds will immediately become a qualified lead. (Wouldn't that be great?) You therefore need to nurture prospects by having new visitors consume your blog posts, podcasts, and videos. By doing that, you are top of mind when they're looking for a solution you can solve.

Lead generation (both inbound leads and outbound leads), then, is how you execute demand-generation goals. No one will go from zero to 100 off the bat when you're selling to them, meaning you have to get that demand going and have people in your team follow up.

The simplest method to get your visitors to step into your funnel is to educate them. You do this through unique, original content on your website. Like blogging, paid advertising attracts visitors through keywords. Unlike blogging, targeted campaigns can reach out beyond Google rankings and your website. LinkedIn advertising is another effective way to target your advertising to the right potential customers.

Lead nurturing is an often-overlooked activity that assists new visitors through the sales pipeline by continuing to contact them through social media channels and email, constantly presenting the next step in the customer journey.

It's now time to assess where you stand within this engine of your business. Here are a few primer questions to get the juices flowing:

1. Do you have an inbound lead-generation process that runs independently of people?

2. Do you have a well-functioning outbound-prospecting process that generates leads based on good intel?

3. Do you systematically nurture leads through the funnel?

The Sales Engine

At its core, this is an embedded sales methodology understood by all, with a clear sales cadence and high-quality customer engagement, resulting in an above-average deal closure rate.

At Bluleader, I had to shift my mindset from consultant to being sales-driven before I had my breakthrough in building a scaled business. For many consultants, "sales" is almost a dirty word, but the fact is, there is no scale without selling. You can continue to keep yourself and a small group of others billable, but to scale, you will require a sales engine.

The sales engine needs to be fed by the demand and lead engines across multiple channels. It comprises several different components that, in unison, are highly effective:

- Salespeople

- Sales process

- Sales systems

- Sales methodology

- Sales meetings

Salespeople

A challenge that all technology services businesses face is how to find and effectively use good salespeople. The first step in this process is to take the plunge within your current team and allocate someone who has the capability to sell. In my case, that was me. I had to get off the tools (foregoing short-term billable revenue) and focus on winning business. I noticed that every time I was focused on selling and not on delivery-related issues, we started to win more work.

Sales Process

This is the process that a lead will follow through the funnel to the point of it being a billable sale. It describes the qualification gates that they pass through. An example sales process is shown below:

1. Prospect

2. Lead qualification

3. Company research

4. Pitch proposal

5. Negotiation

6. Close

There are many variants of this process. This book is not a sales training manual; therefore, I suggest you read about the subject and learn the nuances of a good sales process. Here are a few recommendations for you to peruse in your own time:

The New Strategic Selling: The Unique Sales System Proven Successful by the World's Best Companies by Robert Miller, Stephen Heiman, and Tad Tuleja

The Joshua Principle: Leadership Secrets of Selling by Tony Hughes

The Challenger Sale: Taking Control of the Customer Conversation by Brent Adamson and Matthew Dixon

My message for you, however, is establish a sales process and stick to it doggedly. When the company is small, the question comes up: "Isn't this overkill for a small company?" or "Surely, this is only for large businesses, right?" This is true if you plan to remain small, but remember, we're talking about setting up a scalable business.

Sales Systems

To support the sales process, you need a good customer relationship management (CRM) system. You can start with something as simple as a spreadsheet that allows all leads to be captured and managed in one central repository. Do not delay starting a sales process simply because you do not have a CRM yet. Once you do have a CRM, you can migrate the spreadsheet data into it. With the pervasive nature of cloud solutions, it's easy to obtain cost-effective, feature-rich CRM solutions that meet the needs of a sizable tech services business. I suggest these key features that are critical for scaleexcluding the obvious CRM-type functions):

- Mobile-friendly (salespeople need an intuitive tool)

- Role-based structure (allowing separation of data by salespeople, for when you have a larger team)

- Easy to extract all data if a move to a different system is necessary

- Simple APIs to allow, for example, leads to be auto-generated from another system

- Good pipeline reporting that will be used in sales meetings and team management

Another key component of a sales system is a repository where all sales-related data can be centrally stored. This data is critical business intellectual property (IP) and, as a result, should be trackable, auditable, securely stored, and easy to retrieve. You cannot retain all salespeople over time, but you do want this data to always remain with the business. Once again, with the cloud options now available, this is not hard to achieve.

Sales Methodology

There are many books written about sales methodologies. A sales methodology is a framework or guide for salespeople on how best to approach prospects. The sales methodology will support the sales process to keep all salespeople on brand, on message, and speaking the same language with the aim of increasing win rates and closing more deals. Depending on your organization, types of deals, and customers, there are various "templated" sales methodologies you can embed within your team. Here are just some out of many examples:

- The Challenger Sale

- Solution Selling

- SPIN Selling

- MEDDIC

- Sandler Sales

I suggest researching these (and the others out there) and selecting one that works for you. I do not advocate for one over the other, but I recommend you adopt one that is not too onerous or administratively burdensome and embed this within your sales culture. This needs to become part of your sales DNA.

Sales Meetings

When you are small, a regular sales meeting—once a week—will include whoever is responsible for sales and key staff members with access to clients. Its focus should be tactical in nature. This is not a time to strategize on large sales ideas (there's time for these in specific strategic meetings) but rather an opportunity to review the pipeline (stored in the CRM), come up with tactics to progress stalled opportunities, and ensure the data in the system is accurate. This discipline will start to create a sales mindset within the business and, as the team grows, will become a critical driver of sales focus and success.

Now that you have a basic understanding of the sales engine, take a step back and review how you are performing in this area of your business. You may ask yourself these questions:

1. Do you have a documented and broadly understood sales process?

2. Do you effectively track leads through to opportunities, e.g., via a system or process visible to your staff?

3. Does your current deal pipeline cover your forecast for the next two quarters?

4. Do you know what your market standard bid-to-win ratios are?

The Delivering Work Engines

The Production Engine

The production engine is the delivery operation. It's about delivering high-quality solutions and project outcomes for customers.

In the early stages of the technology services business, you as the owner are both the sales engine and, typically, the delivery engine, especially if you possess the technology skills. This was very much the case for me at Bluleader. Another company, a global organization we knew well in the industry, had someone responsible for setting up the client. He had no hands-on tools knowledge at all, but he could sell. I watched how that company grew and continues to grow exponentially to hundreds of staff. Why is this?

To me, it was clear that he invested in a production engine and, as a result, could focus solely on selling. He allowed his delivery capability to run independently of him, and in doing so, nothing held him back from selling.

The purpose of a production engine is not only to deliver the work as promised—that is obviously very important—it's also to **solve problems**. The whole reason we exist in the tech services industry is that we solve our customers' problems.

David Shein used to tell the customer, "You're going to go through a valley of death before you get to the other side and things will go wrong!" So, you start off with a problem that you're going to solve, and as you solve that problem, you'll encounter more problems. You might even cause some! Therefore, you must be in a position where you can sit over the top and be a point of escalation for the production team. Importantly, you're not the actual delivery person yourself nor do you manage delivery.

To achieve that, you need to have people who own either all of delivery or parts of delivery. Think of it like a hospital. When things go wrong at a hospital, the only way to save lives is to have the right people in place who know how to handle every problem. They also know when they should escalate to the next level, and the next level, as well as what should be escalated right to the top. If you, in your tech services business, have a situation where everything is escalated to you every day and your staff is incapable of solving any problems themselves, you don't have a smooth-functioning production engine in place that allows you to scale.

A well-functioning production engine has **project controls** in place. Project controls are methods of reporting back to you, as an owner, on status. What's the burn rate? What's the estimated time to complete? Are we running into any trouble? Project controls let you identify lead indicators within your production engine to determine each project's results.

Another critical component for success is that your **sales** and your **production** engines are **well connected and well aligned**. In other words, people who are selling are *not* selling something that production cannot deliver. Equally, production does not undermine the sales team's efforts by, for example, not being able to deliver on budget or on time (and by not working with sales on how this should be communicated to the customer), which prevents further sales to that customer.

A well-functioning production engine will also have a knowledge-management system—good processes in place that guarantee every project will harvest as much information as is needed. Future projects and future consultants can then also benefit from the data, which should include lessons learned, tips and tricks, and templates. All these things become a good driver for project success and profitability.

Another critical component of production is that we are measuring **project satisfaction** at the client level, not just overall customer satisfaction. What is the satisfaction level for each project as it's delivered? How is that fed back into the business, and how does it allow you to really improve?

Finally, is there a **clear escalation path** defined between you and your customers? Is there also one between you and your staff for any delivery-related issues? Every small issue should not be coming back to you as an owner. If that is the case, your production processes and your escalation path have not been well structured and well defined.

Similarly, you don't want to find out that things that should have been escalated to you were not. It needs to be clear to you and to the customer when you have delivery-related issues and what the correct delivery-escalation path is so that you can achieve great customer satisfaction.

Here are some primer questions to ask yourself to see if your production engine is operating at peak efficiency:

1. Do you schedule resources on a well-planned basis, as opposed to reactively?

2. Is your sales pipeline connected to your resource pipeline?

3. Do you have a well-functioning customer-escalation process?

The Back-Office Engine

Having a solid back-office engine means the visibility of business performance runs seamlessly and the "money in, money out" element of the business is well managed. This engine is all about finance and revenue.

It's probably the least cool of the lot, but without it operating effectively, you will run out of cash and have upset, incorrectly paid staff, unhappy vendors, and the tax department on your heels, which will surely result in disaster. A well-oiled back-office engine runs without fanfare in the background and will ensure a thriving business continues as such. When you start the business, it will likely be you or another owner (or family member) who performs these activities on the side. This means the role is not normally done as well as it should be. There are two key elements that will help you here and allow you to scale in this area.

Firstly, as with all of the engines, it's about having the right person or people on the team. The challenge here will be identifying that person to recruit. Do you start with a generalist all-rounder or a few specialists? Do they need to know your industry?

At Bluleader, we started with a generalist office admin person but found they were not as equipped to handle the accounting and payroll side of things. We then moved to an outsourced book-keeper who knew the IT services industry. We paid her hourly, as we only needed a part-time person in the first few years. She was great for that time, as she understood time sheet billing, payroll, and IT services accounting.

As we grew, and the workload increased, we realized we needed to bring the function into a full-time role. We then recruited an experienced, semiretired accountant. We took a chance on him as he did not have much experience of working in our industry, but he had a great attitude, was thorough, and was clearly very loyal, based on his career history. He stayed with us all the way until our exit. I would rate him as one of the best employees I've ever seen!

The point here is that it's not always easy to define this role. I suggest you find the person or people who broadly meet your criteria and then shape the role around their particular skills. For example, if they are strong in bookkeeping and payroll but are weaker in the monthly timesheet billing, invest in a good auto-mated timesheet billing solution to support them. By playing to people's strengths and using efficient systems, we were able to run our back-office functions for a team of 100 people using only two administrative staff members!

Secondly, your systems should be automated and scalable. As we move into the age of artificial intelligence, solutions have developed greatly compared to when we started. What's more, they are affordable. The key back-office solution features should cover financial forecasting, timesheet capture (spreadsheets will scale very well for this task), time billing, financial reporting, payroll, and basic management accounting (cost center and project level). These functions can be covered by one system, such as a professional service automation (PSA) tool, which can be costly to purchase on setup. The other option is to use a few solutions that you manually interface, i.e., export and import files. Therefore, you can, for example, have a timesheet solution, an accounting system, and reporting tool that, in the early days, are nonintegrated. Then, as the business grows, you can integrate these to drive greater automation.

To assess your back-office engine, you should ask yourself some technical, business-related questions. If you're having trouble answering them, it may be time to act fast and employ the strategies above.

1. Do you have real-time access to EBITDA, utilization, revenue per consultant, project gross margin, customer margin, etc.?

2. Do you forecast? Are your forecasts accurate?

3. Do you know what backlog is required for your business?

4. Do you need to adjust fewer than 5 percent of your invoices?

The People Engine

The people engine is all about … well, people! It consists of building a pipeline of future employees and nurturing them, creating an onboarding program that makes them feel special, and building a culture where no one would ever want to leave.

People are the key resource in tech services businesses, yet for many, this area is taken for granted and not handled strategically. Rather, it tends to be reactive based on client demands. The people engine should be treated similarly to the sales engine in that potential candidates are the leads and are constantly nurtured, from joining through to thriving within your business.

Recruitment Funnel

At some point, a massive mindset shift needs to occur within the leadership of a tech services business: You need to shift the pressure from recruitment to sales. There always will be a tension to manage between the amount of work you have sold and the number of people available to deliver this work.

Recruitment has a much higher impact on the overall business than many imagine. If your sales engine is running strongly, there will be pressure on the recruitment team to "resource up." The ideal situation you are aiming for is a strong, well-nurtured people pipeline that you can draw on quickly as deals close. To do this, you must start filling the recruitment funnel well in advance of the sales deals. The more niche-focused your business, the easier this is to do, as it will be clear what types of people you need in the funnel. For a company that is very generalist in approach, however, the recruitment function becomes reactive and therefore more difficult to manage. This leads to higher contractor ratios, higher staff turnover, and less than optimal culture.

Onboarding

Once you have agreed to hire someone, the onboarding process starts. You are running a people-based business, so the onboarding process is an opportunity to "wow" new staff. You only have one chance for every new staff member, so make sure that it's a phenomenal experience. Ensure strong communication throughout the process—make the person feel special and valued.

Career Development

This might sound like MBA 101, but be aware that professional development opportunities are extra important in tech services. Most employees in tech services believe they have an edge over other people in other careers. They also believe the moves they make have big impacts on their ability to produce income and enjoy their jobs. FOMO (fear of missing out) and the abundance of options risk having a paralyzing effect on some staff. If you help them formulate a career plan and then hold them accountable to it, they will overcome their FOMO, remain focused, and thrive.

Don't be concerned about your staff outgrowing your company. If you take care of their careers and support them in their dreams that stretch beyond their employment with you, they will love you for it and repay you in full. Not only will they stay longer, but when they finally move on, they will become an ambassador for you—they might even become your customer.

Culture

Creating a great culture will ensure that staff will not want to leave and that they will be high performers. This is not always easy to do in a technology services business, as a large amount of time is spent with the customer and less with the broader company.

This places an even greater onus on you to be intentional about driving a strong culture. We previously looked at this in detail in chapter 11.

Contractor-to-Permanent Staff Ratio

I'd be remiss if I didn't touch on contractors in this section. What is the correct ratio to maintain between contractors and permanent employees? Is it even important? Many consultancies measure this ratio and even use it as a selling point when promoting the business. Why is this so?

If you're planning to exit through a trade sale of the business, a buyer will be very interested in this metric. They will want to ensure they are buying a "real" business, with employees. Therefore, a lower percentage of contractors is more attractive. On the other hand, for the business owner, contractors provide flexibility when there is a business turndown as you can reduce costs much more easily.

In an ideal world where there is an unlimited demand for your services, would you choose to have a contractor workforce or permanent staff? Permanent is better in all respects—better margins, better control over allocation to work, and better culture. So, the dependency here is on the demand side. The key is, therefore, to ensure that you are consistently winning work that allows for a well-planned recruitment engine to hire permanent staff. The factors that will allow for this to happen are:

- A niche focus—work will come to you if you are known for being the best in your field

- "Always-on" demand and lead engines

- A strong sales engine that generates pressure to hire

Based on these elements, the ideal ratio is 100 percent permanent staff. This figure is obviously highly aspirational as there are always factors, such as unexpected or urgent demands or changes to peoples' personal lives (wanting to switch to a contractor structure, for example), but it can always be the target for the business.

Let's put your culture to the test and ask some tough questions about your people engine. Remember, this is all about attracting qualified candidates, retaining top talent, and creating an environment where they want to perform well.

1. Do you have a clear process for recruitment?

2. Is the average duration from onboarding to billing less than one month?

3. Do your people have a career path, and does your company focus on making this happen?

4. Are you rated as a great place to work by candidates, and does this create a hiring demand?

The Leadership Engines

The Scale Engine

Now we're getting down to brass tacks. If you don't keep scale top of mind, you'll remain complacent. Fortunately, there is an engine entirely dedicated to the proven method and process for replication, which will scale the business without sidetracking other engines.

This engine is about **horizontal scaling**. The previous seven engines all help you to scale vertically, which means bigger deals, more deals, longer-lasting deals, more employees, etc. However, at some point, you might saturate your own market, at which point horizontal scaling is a good option.

I always recommend setting up multiple **profit centers (P&Ls)** as soon as possible. Even if you are a company of only 10 people, I suggest setting up two P&Ls. Learn how they function, and learn the process to make them work. By doing so, you've equipped yourself for the future, where you can add a third and a fourth P&L because you know the process and understand how to grow them.

At Bluleader, we based our practices around areas of **competency** or capability. For example, we would have a CRM practice and an e-commerce practice. Each practice would have a practice manager who would be responsible for the **profitability** of the practice as well as for the **resources** within that practice. They were highly incentivized to grow that practice. We grew from three, then to four, and then to five practices, and we would have carried on at this rate had we not been acquired at this point. We proved that this is an effective way of scaling your business horizontally.

I'm not going to lie to you: getting your scale engine up and running could prove difficult in the beginning. If you've never run multiple P&Ls before, there's going to be a learning curve. Putting the right systems in place, managing the people launching new P&Ls … it'll be hard work. Once you've got it all going, though, you'll never look back. It's the best way to grow your business down the line. It's also important to remember that products come and go, so the thing that you specialize in might be hot right now, but in a few years' time, it might not be as hot, or it might be replaced entirely by a more advanced solution. So, that ability to always be ahead and invest in new technologies is essential.

Do not mistake this diversification for moving out of your niche. What I am referring to here is how to **expand** your offering **within your niche**. How can you further enhance your offerings so that you're seen more as a **specialist**, providing your customer with additional services that are still within your niche while your customer still views you as a specialist in your field? If you can get this right, you have a highly effective way of creating a scale engine.

So, as we have done in each of the prior sections, let's dive into some thought starters about your current ability to scale so you can rate your current state.

1. Do you have a repeatable method for launching new P&Ls within your business?

2. To what extent can your staff close deals and deliver them without your involvement?

3. Do you have a consistent set of measurable KPIs for profit center success?

4. Are goals and measurements well aligned within the company?

The Mastermind Engine

A mastermind makes clear, tactical, and strategic decisions that ensure the business is always on course, irrespective of external factors. Napoleon Hill popularized this term in the 1920s in his book *The Law of Success*. He went on to do further research on this topic, eventually documenting it in *Think and Grow Rich*. At that time, his was the most intensive research on the topic out there.

It was focused on how successful people succeed—as in the most successful people in the world. He found that, without exception, each of these people was part of a mastermind or mastermind group.

While the origin of the definition is unknown, Hill is often attributed with defining a "mastermind" as "the coordination of knowledge and effort of two or more people who work toward a definite purpose in the Spirit of Harmony." The quote is further elaborated with "no two minds ever come together without thereby creating a third invisible, intangible force, which may be likened to a **third invisible mind**."[36]

Hill believed that a mastermind group could help people achieve their goals by providing support, encouragement, and accountability, and it should consist of individuals who share similar goals and have a positive, can-do attitude. The group should meet regularly to discuss their progress and offer feedback and advice to one another.

Fellow author Dale Carnegie was a proponent of Hill's mastermind concept and incorporated it into his own teachings on success and personal development. He believed that a mastermind group could help individuals overcome their fears and limitations and achieve their full potential.

To create a high-functioning business, then, you will need to create this final engine: a group of people who will drive business strategy throughout the journey from sweat to scale. This team is highly likely not static as you will find that different inputs are needed at different stages of the business. Also note that the mastermind is needed from day one—not only when you are a larger business. When you are smaller, you will be able to function with a small mastermind that you call upon only when needed, but the group should still be in place—you will need its input. Do not be shy to invest in a mastermind. It could save you countless hours, headaches, and money! The types of members included in a mastermind are:

The Dream Team (Normally External to the Business)

- **Accountant.** This is not the accountant who works day-to-day on your books but a specialist or specialists external to the business who will advise you on things like tax structures and accounting best practices. Having this set up correctly lets you avoid many unforeseen financial surprises and will also facilitate an eventual sale of the business.

- **Commercial lawyer.** Advisors of this nature may seem costly, but they can save you much heartache and costs in the long run. At different stages of your journey, you will need critical legal input. When you set the business up, invest in defining a shareholders' agreement. Create well-structured employment and contractor agreements. It might be tempting to simply copy one from elsewhere or download one from the web, but remember, these agreements will be in place for years, so they are worth thinking through and setting up correctly. You will likely also need legal input when you sign key customer contracts as well as when you sell the business.

It's important too that the correct legal advisor is sought for different scenarios. For example, the lawyer who drew up our employment contracts was not the same lawyer who worked with us on the sale of the business. As a side note, although I recommend strong legal input, be aware that the lawyer does not have the final word—they are an input to your decision-making process. There will be times where you must make a commercial call not aligned with your lawyer. They are risk averse by nature!

- **Human resources specialist.** You might run into HR-related challenges that could escalate to legal challenges. A specialist in HR can be of great assistance navigating through some of these sensitive issues.

- **Broker or banker.** Ensure a good business relationship with your banks because access to finance and smooth banking processes is an essential component in growing your business. Insist on more than just a relationship with a teller. Instead, aim for a business manager at the bank or a strong business finance broker, as these relationships come in handy at key stages of scaling.

- **The Board.** When the business is small, a board may seem unnecessary. But a board will establish a shareholder agreement and define the company constitution. I believe that the board plays more than a legal or bureaucratic role. If utilized correctly, it can be very powerful in driving good strategy.

- **Directors.** Having a board of directors that would normally consist of the shareholders and possibly nonexecutive members who meet regularly (monthly or quarterly) will ensure a strong, consistent focus on business direction. Note that the board should not focus on tactical day-to-day items but rather on big-ticket strategic decisions. When Bluleader first started, we had a board on paper, but it did not really function as intended. As we grew, encountered ownership challenges, and faced big strategic decisions, Millionaire Mentor and I structured a board that functioned as we needed it to. By doing so, we managed to drive some pivotal and significant changes into the business that became a catalyst for a real acceleration of the company. I know that without this focus on the board and good business governance, we would never have achieved what we did. The board gave me, as managing director, the critical direction and support I needed as we drove the business forward.

- **Non-executive advisor or coaches.** At different stages of your business's evolution, external advisors who do not work within the business can be invaluable. They bring a fresh perspective as well as learnings gained elsewhere that can be revolutionary. These appointments do not need to be static but can change according to your business's shifting needs. For example, in the early stages, you might have a coach who helps with strategy and high-performing teams. As the business evolves, you might get a specialist in who has grown businesses through acquisitions (if this is your strategy).

Key Leaders Within the Business

Another element of the mastermind that can add great value is key staff within the business. These are not shareholders or directors but rather people in the business with a strategic mindset. It's very important here that these are members of the team who can separate their strategic thinking from day-to-day activities, are positive, are seen by others as leaders, and are committed to the company vision. They can be from any level of the business, but in tech services, they typically tend to be practice leads. I would caution against having salespeople as part of this mastermind as they are very single-minded, i.e., sales above all, as is expected of them.

When evaluating your mastermind engine, set your ego aside, so you can objectively identify all the different types of leaders and specialists who can help you along the way. You may ask yourself some of these questions as a part of assessing if your mastermind is working adequately:

1. Are you able to act as a leader/visionary more than a doer/firefighter?

2. Can your company make innovative strategic decisions (not including day-to-day decisions here) and be nimble enough to change rapidly?

3. Do employees have high confidence in the leadership team and, therefore, the mastermind?

4. Are you basing big decisions solely on information within the business, or are you referring to broader external information too?

To close, although the business mastermind is a stand-alone engine, each of the eight "always-on" engines should contain its own mini mastermind. Normally, this is someone who leads the engine—a team member who executes the functions and membership as prescribed by the business mastermind, such as a director, shareholder, etc. Appointing these team members within each engine will ensure further efficiency and preparation for scale.

Now that you've learned about the ideal state of each of the eight "always-on" engines, it's time to rate your business in these areas. Again, you can use the baseline questions above as a diving board, but a better way to assess the efficiency of these engines in your business in the greatest detail is to take my online assessment, which will give you a numerical grade of your current state.

To take the online assessment, visit sweat2scale.com.

You'll use these numbers on your A3 Strategy, which is the turn-key method to strategically plan your business for massive scale and growth within the next one to five years. In the next section, you'll learn exactly how to fill out the A3 Strategy using all of the intel you've gathered from this section.

Key Takeaways

1. There are eight engines that should be "always on" and never slowed down by another engine. This is how your business will grow in a scalable way with less and less involvement from you.

2. There are three engine categories: Winning Work, Delivering Work, and Leadership.

3. Within the Winning Work category, there are three engines: Demand, Lead, and Sales.

4. Within the Delivering Work category, there are three more engines: Production, Back-Office, and People.

5. Within the Leadership category, there are two final engines: Scaling and Mastermind.

6. Rate yourself within each of the engines by taking my online assessment at sweat2scale.com.

PART IV

EXECUTION

CHAPTER 16

The A3 Strategy

It's time to put your thinking cap on as I introduce you to the A3 Strategy.

This step-by-step approach for going from sweat to scale is so called because all of the necessary elements of the strategy can be captured and fit onto one A3-size page. It should be visible to you at all times and guide your decisions on a day-to-day basis.

Disclaimer: *While the A3 Strategy can and should be shared with all employees at your company, you should* not *share your exit strategy with anyone but your shareholders. Employees may be uneasy when seeing and thinking about your goals to eventually sell.*

More holistically, everything you need to know about your business goes on this one page. This is the secret to transforming yourself from being a techie who puts food on the table for your family to a businessperson who looks at a much bigger picture. That bigger picture is the A3 Strategy.

In parts II and III, we discussed the MATE Framework—Mindset, Active and Target States, and Execution, the "always-on" engines that run your business. These elements all appear on the A3 Strategy. In this chapter I will outline the step-by-step process of filling out your A3 Strategy. Then, in the chapters that follow, we will work through how to execute your plan.

A3 STRATEGY TEMPLATE

M	A	T	E			
Mindset	**Active State**	**Target State**	**Execution**			
Core Values and Beliefs	Perceived Competencies	BHAG	Initiatives 3-5 Years	**8 Execution Engines**		
Purpose	Value Proposition	Perceived Competencies		The Demand Engine	The Production Engine	
	Market	Value Proposition	Current Year Initiatives	The Lead Engine	The Back-Office Engine	
	SWOT	Market				
	Strengths	Targets 3-5 Years		The Sales Engine	The People Engine	
	Weakness					
	Opportunities	Goals 1 Year		The Mastermind Engine	The Scaling Engine	
	Threats					

Go to the Resources page on www.sweat2scale.com for a free download of the A3 Strategy Template

4 Quarter Execution					
		Quarter 1	Quarter 2	Quarter 3	Quarter 4
Dates					
Revenue					
EBIT					
Gross Margin					
Utilization					
Coverage					
Pipeline Yield					
DSO					
Revenue per Employee					
Anchors					
1	Description				
	Who				
2	Description				
	Who				
3	Description				
	Who				
4	Description				
	Who				
5	Description				
	Who				

*Go to the Resources page on www.sweat2scale.com for a free
download of the A3 Strategy Template*

Step 1: BHAG and Target State

You may be thinking, "Marco, why am I starting in the middle of
this document?" The reason is that you must identify where you
want to be and map the delta between that point and where you
are now (your Active State). This will help you determine which
engines you need to invest in over the next quarter, next few quarters, or the next year to move you closer to your BHAG.

For example, you may say, "One of the biggest obstacles to getting to our Target State is that our numbers are not good enough. We have a good delivery team and our production is great, but we don't have enough leads or sales coming in." Firstly, then, you write down the need to increase the energy expended in your lead and sales engines, even if you can't hire 10 more people just yet. This takes careful planning and budget management to work. More on that in the next chapter.

For now, complete the Target State section, starting with your BHAG and working your way backward. Remember the exercises we did in chapters 12 and 14—be real about where you are now and where you want to be. This section should be filled out with *your ideal company* in mind, laying out your goals for the next one to five years.

This model means that you should be able to cascade these steps down throughout your business. For example, a practice manager will own one part of the strategy and, in turn, will have her own A4 Strategy (on a smaller page, hence "A4") for her team, with all the same elements, minus any actions around the engines.

Step 2: Mindset and Active State

Now you can go back and fill out the sections that relate to the here and now. First, look at the Mindset section, which contains your core values, your beliefs, and your purpose. These are the mentalities you should embody and keep in mind when growing your business, perpetuating healthy company culture down through your employees.

Next, fill out the Active State section. Remember, this is where you are right now—not where you think you are right now but where you truthfully are. This is based on the results of your assessment and the research and outreach you've done both within your organization and with your customers.

Step 3: Rate Your Engines

If you haven't already, run an assessment of your business to see where you stand with each of your eight engines. Take the online assessment at sweat2scale.com, which gives you numerical scores you can use to track against and build upon as you grow toward your goals. Take the scores from your assessment and record them here, and note down what you need to do to improve those scores over time.

Step 4: Set Your Long-Term Goals and Initiatives

Based on your targets and goals in the Target State section, move on to the Execution section to fill out your long-term initiatives (three to five years) and your current-year initiatives (one year).

Your current-year initiatives should directly correlate with your 3- to 5-year initiatives. These are the building blocks to success. Then, when you reach the next step, you'll be prepared and able to determine the necessary goals that will lead you to reaching your current-year initiatives.

Step 5: Fill Out the Four-Quarter Execution

Now you'll plan your current year, breaking down your 1-year goals into quarterly goals. This covers everything from financials to sales pipeline to individual anchors that will drive your measurable KPIs.

If you use the cascading methodology of taking a big goal, breaking it down into smaller goals, and working backward, it will be easy for you to stay on track. However, if you try to create goals for your current state first, you may lead yourself astray and will not actually be working toward your 1- to 5-year goals.

The A3 Strategy may seem overwhelming at first. That's why it's important to break it down into smaller chunks. I'll guide you along the way. The chapters that follow outline the day-to-day execution steps that will transform your A3 Strategy from a working document to a living, breathing reality.

Key Takeaways

1. The A3 Strategy captures all the necessary elements onto one A3-size page. It should be visible to you at all times and guide your decisions on a day-to-day basis.

2. The elements of the MATE Framework (Mindset, Active and Target States, and Execution) all appear on the A3 Strategy.

3. You start the A3 Strategy process by determining your BHAG and Target State.

4. The A3 Strategy is created via an off-site session with your other owners and key leaders in the business.

CHAPTER 17

How to Keep Your Engines Running

Now that you've got your A3 Strategy filled out and all your teams on board, it's time to ensure that your engines are "always on," even when you are not around. Remember, the key is to get you off the tools and solely focused on growing and scaling your business toward your end goal, such as an exit strategy.

In addition to using the A3 Strategy to stay on track, let's discuss some specific techniques that will ensure each engine is kept "always on."

Demand-Generation Engine

Leverage Consultants

Use the wealth of knowledge and expertise that lives within your consultants and employees. Create a culture within the organization of continual content creation. This content should be the result of project go-lives or solutions deployed. It should first be presented internally to the broader company team, then repurposed into multiple forms of media, like whitepapers, blogs, or video. These can then be distributed to social media channels, once again leveraging staff to share and distribute the content, which will create a sense of ownership of company intellectual property as well as a sense of pride within the team.

Repurpose

Always consider how artifacts or outputs can be repurposed into some form of content. For example, a design-thinking workshop with a customer might create some great materials, so ensure you photograph the session, retain examples of outputs, and then produce an anonymized article (so as not to not divulge client-confidential information) showing how your business can create value for your customers.

Customers

Involve customers in your demand-generation activities. At Bluleader, we attained high-quality demand-generation events (in our case, breakfast sessions) that were focused on existing customers speaking to prospective customer attendees about the value we delivered for them. The existing customer benefits as it raises their personal and business brands and allows for them to network with their peers. These sessions can be recorded and repurposed into articles and other content that continues for months after the event. I recommend agreeing with new customers up front when first contracting with them that when you have delivered a successful outcome, they will be a reference who might speak at an event, do a video case study, or endorse you when pursuing another deal.

Create an Annual Demand Calendar

Every year, create a demand-generation plan. This will detail down to a quarterly and weekly basis what content is to be produced. Demand generation will always play second fiddle to urgent crises that come up daily in a tech services business. Sticking to and monitoring your plan weekly will help to retain focus on this important activity. Also be realistic in terms of what the plan will deliver, concentrating on fewer high-value deliverables rather than on a large quantity of low-value ones. Always remember that a person (prospective customer) should want to consume what is being created and will expect value from the artifact produced.

Lead-Generation Engine

Software

Technology can be used as an enabler of lead generation, allowing you to keep it running without constant people involvement. The use of a good marketing automation tool is powerful for:

- **Lead capture.** Offer a piece of content online and ask for contact information, thereby systematically capturing leads. The content, known as a "lead magnet," needs to be of high value to the prospect to ensure they provide contact details.

- **Landing pages.** Click-through landing pages attract the visitor to a specific offering or service you're trying to sell (such as an invite to a webinar or a particular offer). Landing pages have one call-to-action—they do not overwhelm visitors with information regarding your business and all the products and services you offer.

- **Lead scoring.** Automation of the lead-scoring process enables the marketing tool to automatically route the scores to the correct people, therefore eliminating much human intervention.

- **Broader team involvement.** Before you have sales staff in your business, ascertain who from your team can perform parts of the sales process, like lead nurturing. Leads captured through your automated systems can be contacted by your staff with good people skills or understanding of the solutions. This exposes your team to the sales process and creates a culture of "all of us are sellers." It also exposes your customers to some of your best people.

Sales Engine

The regular sales meeting is the absolute best way to keep the sales engine running on a consistent basis. This regular cadence of accountability will ensure everyone sticks to the road map and keeps meeting expectations.

Additionally, a well-run sales engine will record opportunities in a **system** and give good visibility of how those opportunities are **tracking**. Appoint people to be responsible for these opportunities, then discuss them in your regular meetings, and track how you're pushing them through the funnel until they're closed.

Your sales engine should also be producing good **metrics**. Ideally, your ratios are better than the market's. If the market standard is one in three bids are won, and you're achieving one in two, you're doing very well. Another way to generate good results is not having to discount on deals and the ability to sell at full margin.

Production Engine

Hire the Correct Delivery Leads

In my mind, there are two key roles that will make or break the production engine. The first is the manager or lead of the particular delivery capability or practice. This manager should have good skills in the technology or solution being delivered but not the strongest in the practice. Their core strength is to be one of building, managing, and growing a team. They will need to have good commercial knowledge and strong client-facing skills. This person is key to the "always-on" capability that owners can allow to run with little input other than monitoring results closely.

The second key role is the right-hand person to the manager. This should be the strongest person on the particular technology in the practice. Together, these are a highly effective combination that can hire exceptional team members, assess complex client issues, and deliver successfully with very little input from anyone outside this team. This structure can feasibly grow to a 15- to 20-person practice and deliver high quality.

Define Methodology/Process

Some might argue that you cannot build practices until you have methodology and process already bedded down. I would counter that the practice structure itself can often define much of the methodology within that practice, which can then be expanded into a template for future practices. If you wait until the delivery methodologies are complete before starting the production engine, you will find that there is no time to focus on growth because you've spent so long on the start-up. A key to these businesses is to never let perfection hinder action!

Project and Delivery Management

This is particularly challenging to achieve when your projects are smaller or shorter in duration. At Bluleader, we certainly saw higher success rates in projects when we started to sell in a project management role onto the work we delivered. You don't necessarily need to permanently hire these project managers (PMs), but you should have a pool of trusted PMs you can call upon when required. You can also contract a PM to help you define a project delivery methodology and framework on an internal project. Good PMs will bring with them a toolbox of accelerators, templates, and recommendations on methodologies and ensure high levels of customer satisfaction and an ongoing funnel of references. My experience is that leaving this to the lead consultants to perform almost never works (unless you have a lead who is a great PM, which is rare).

Back-Office Engine

Some of the critical measures required in a services business that need to be monitored vigilantly by the back-office engine are

- the bench—when your billing staff members are not billing customers,

- project profitability, and

- contractor compliance.

This was a key learning in my journey growing Bluleader. In the beginning, these measures were not prioritized, but over time, I realized how crucial they are to business success.

Interplay of Bench and Project Profitability

Utilization has a disproportionate impact on the profitability and cash flow of a services business—even more so within a technology services business where staff costs are so high, meaning any nonbillable time has a large impact on the bottom line. This is not to say that striving for 100 percent billability is the goal either, as this would mean very little investment in people's careers or skills development, resulting in a gradual decline in quality and culture.

So, what is the optimum utilization level? This really depends on how your business is structured and the kind of work you deliver, but it can be calculated by doing a bottom-up calculation. Below, we can see how $100 of revenue sold to a customer might be broken down for an example services business:

	$
Total sales	100
Minus Cost of sale (direct staff costs)	60
Equals Gross Margin	40
Minus Bench cost	10
Minus Business Overheads	15
Equals Remaining net profit	15

In this case, based on the business cost structure and margins created on deals, a bench cost of 10 percent of revenue would allow the business to achieve a 15 percent EBIT. Using this as an example, assuming a typical consultant bills out at $1,500 per day and can realistically bill 220 days per year (after public holidays, sick leave, and annual vacation), they can generate $330,000 per year. If that person's direct cost to the company is $198,000 per year (60 percent of $330,000), then to reach the EBIT targets, 10 percent of $330,000 is the amount of time they can have "on the bench," i.e., 22 days. This would translate to a target utilization of 90 percent.

If a lower utilization is targeted for this person, and the EBIT is to be maintained, their "sell" rate needs to be higher, their salary needs to be lower, or overhead costs need to be managed. This calculation is oversimplified here when viewed purely at a single-person level but when carried out at an overall team level where better margin spreads can occur, it effectively illustrates how to arrive at the correct target margins and utilization levels.

These measures need to be easily and readily visible out of the data that the back-office engine generates so that the pulse of the business is kept in check.

Contractor Compliance

Contractor management is another trap within a tech services business that can cause a large amount of unexpected pain. As the business grows and demand for people increases, you will likely start using more contractors. When this happens, the tendency is to treat contractor tax and other statutory requirements rather loosely. This is dangerous as there are some expensive traps here that can have a retrospectively negative impact on your business. Depending on where you are based, look out for these items:

- Payroll taxes

- Retirement provisions

- Income tax implications

Ensure that you get good legal and accounting advice on how to correctly structure contractors, and ensure the back-office engine manages this very carefully. It's critical that this area is well handled and documented when you get to a sale of the business, as it's an area of high scrutiny for potential buyers.

People Engine

We've already discussed in detail the building blocks to hiring and retaining top talent and giving them career goals to incentivize them to stay. However, as I outlined much earlier in the book, culture is of utmost importance. To foster an outstanding culture and keep your people engine humming, focus on four steps:

Define the Business Purpose and
Unite Everyone Behind It

A company's purpose must be well defined and communicated consistently to staff. It should be lofty and not about money or profit. This is normally written as a mission statement. Some examples of mission statements of leading companies in the world are:

- *"To make it easy to do business anywhere"*—Alibaba Group

- *"To be a company that inspires and fulfills your curiosity"*—Sony

- *"Improving people's lives through meaningful innovation"*—Philips

- *"To move the web forward and give web designers and developers the best tools and services in the world"*—Adobe

As you can see, these statements are lofty and designed to give staff members a sense of higher purpose they can unite behind.

Maintain Clear, Strong Practice Niches
That Create a Sense of Belonging

People who have common skills and goals within a team or practice feel connected and are motivated to learn from one another. An obvious example of this is in sports teams where members share common skills, purpose, and some healthy competition.

Focus on Leadership Meeting Face-to-Face with Staff

Be very careful that you do not lose touch with your employees as the business grows. Aim to foster a forum or environment in which face-to-face interaction of leadership with staff occurs regularly. I have personally seen culture destroyed when the CEO of a fast-growing company works out of a large, fancy office separate from staff and creates a barrier (real or perceived) to staff connection.

Bring the Company Together Regularly

Be intentional in creating events in which teams can be brought together in one place. This comes at a cost to billable revenue but is actually a much smaller cost in the long run than the fallout from a bad company culture. These events will ensure staff retention as well as being a way to attract potential staff in the market when you post on social media platforms celebrating your culture.

Scaling Engine

To truly scale a technology services business, you need engines of revenue that can run with minimal involvement from you as an owner. The key to scale is being the best within your niche and then finding an effective way of replicating this.

Jim Collins, in his famous book *Good to Great*, talks about understanding your economic denominator. This concept provides insight into what your company's economic drivers are and therefore will give you a method for driving replication. The economic denominator is defined as a single ratio, e.g., profit per X or cash flow per X that you can *systematically* increase over time and that will be the key driver of your economic success.[40]

As an example, Walgreens changed its economic denominator from profit per store to profit per customer visit. This allowed them to increase customer convenience (their niche was being the best at <u>convenient</u> drug stores) by having more stores in an area. Using the old denominator of profit per store would have meant that by having more stores close together, profit per store would decline, which would have been a negative measure. Using the new denominator, they could scale and measure success correctly.

A key to the scale engine, then, is finding that correct denominator. Ask yourself what the correct cellular-level building block is for your business and then define the appropriate measure to use. For Walgreens, the cellular-level building block was the store, which was measured by profit per customer visit. For a tech services business, these are some typical examples:

TYPICAL PRACTICE TYPES

Cellular Building Block	Description	Example Economic Ratio
The Competency Practice	The business is broken into practices by grouping teams by competency type, e.g., networking practice, cyber practice.	Percentage gross margin per practice, average profit per employee in the practice

Cellular Building Block	Description	Example Economic Ratio
Geographical Practices	The business is broken up by geographical area. This makes sense where competencies are very homogeneous across the business.	Percentage profit per area, average profit per employee in the practice
Key Client/Client Group Practices	Where there are large key clients or client groups (e.g., industries), the building block might be based on a client grouping.	Percentage profit per customer, percentage of profit contribution to company profit

One of the most effective ways of creating a cellular-structured business is to create practices with their own profit and loss (P&L) responsibility. Each practice will have a manager who is rewarded for the profits that the practice generates. With the correct people, settings, size, and high-functioning grouping mechanisms, these practices are a great way to achieve scale.

Practice Size

This is an important factor to get right when setting up a practice, as it will help you to understand a logical grouping and what kind of practice manager you will need. I have found that the optimal practice size is around the 20-person mark. At this size, it is possible to have good, shared relationships within the team and good access to the practice manager, yet it's not too large to want to run as a totally independent company, i.e., with its own marketing or administrative functions. This means the practice can have a strong practice culture as well as a strong alignment to the company culture. This size also allows for the practice manager to be well remunerated.

Grouping Mechanisms

The first decision to make when setting up a practice is to consider the grouping criteria, i.e., capability based, function based, or geographical. Evaluate your grouping mechanisms on a case-by-case basis within the context of your operations, keeping in mind a target team of around the 20-person mark. Bluleader, for example, was a business focused on the implementation of customer engagement software, i.e., sales, service, marketing, and e-commerce So we looked at these areas and decided how best to group common capabilities and align them with that technology. What we found was that sales, service, and marketing technology utilized common skill sets, whereas e-commerce was quite distinct. There was also a component of specialized, bespoke development that utilized yet a different set of tools and skills. Therefore, we formed three customer-engagement practices, i.e., Practice 1: Sales, Service, and Marketing, Practice 2: E-Commerce and Practice 3: Edge/Bespoke Development.

Setting Up and Challenges to Be Addressed

Remuneration. For the practice manager who is commercially minded, remuneration incentives to drive great performance will be very important. As their role is to grow revenue and profit, my view is that they should be incentivized on the profit that their practice generates. This can be a percentage of the profit (profit share) or bonuses based on hitting certain profit goals. The key here is to document, define, and agree upon all the components that make up practice revenue, costs, and therefore, resulting profit. If not well documented and agreed upon, there may be unnecessary discord that can undermine the effectiveness of the practice. It's also critical to be able to track all these measures at least on a monthly basis.

Cross charges/areas of responsibility. In setting up the practices, delineation of work responsibility and resultant revenue recognition are very important considerations, because, as the practices grow, unforeseen areas of overlap will arise. Have a mechanism to deal with these issues before they occur. A simple documented method can be a set of rules of engagement that define how revenue will be divided up when an initiative delivered to a customer is performed by more than one practice. At Bluleader, we had a rule that the percentage or absolute value splits were agreed between the practice managers at a project's outset.

No company alignment. As practices grow in size, they can have a tendency to want to be on an "island" of capability. It's great that a practice culture is strong and that they can run predominantly on their own, but they should always have a sense of being a part of the overall company. To maintain this balance, follow these guidelines:

- Don't let the practice grow much larger than 20 people— it's better to spin out a second practice.

- Don't allow the practice to develop its own shared service or back-office function; rather, it should leverage the business's shared services, such as marketing, accounting, and administration.

- Create system architectural forums that allow for cross-practice initiatives and knowledge sharing across the company.

Mastermind Engine

The **mastermind** is an amazing thing when you get it right. In a tech services firm, you must first find people outside your business who can advise you and help you form your mastermind. These should be **people you trust** who have **walked the path you're walking**.

You also want to include some people from inside your company. They might have done more things in the industry than you have, or they might have less experience than you but are full of great ideas. Don't choose people who are negative—people who feel paralyzed by the day-to-day challenges and activities that happen within the business. You need people in the mastermind who can rise above the noise, **think creatively**, and motivate the team—people who are strategic in their thinking.

Your mastermind should be able to get together **at least once a month** and forget about the daily pains of the business.

Getting it right is the closest guarantee you'll have **of reaching the goals** you have set for yourself.

Time to Grow

People may ask you, "What's your growth strategy?" The word "growth" is abstract and can mean many things. As an alternative, I suggest the term "cloning strategy." It's basically an expansion strategy with a high probability of success.

When Tesla launched its first mass production car, the Model S, they built an assembly line that would produce clones of the first real Model S. These cars are, for all practical purposes, perfect clones of each other. This cloning process means that Tesla can produce a steady flow of cars. But once the assembly line reaches its maximum capacity, the steady flow of cars stagnates, and production hits a wall. This is perhaps what's happening in your business today.

Tesla then lifted its game and implemented a cloning strategy at a higher level, i.e., it cloned the assembly line itself. It went on to open new factories with more assembly lines, then it manufactured in more countries with more assembly lines. The key entity to be cloned here is not the car but the assembly line.

However, growth in supply does not automatically translate to growth in demand, e.g., if a struggling car company started aggressively cloning its assembly lines, it wouldn't be able to sell the cars if there were no demand.

So far, we've talked about supply. But it's also possible to put a demand-generation process in place and then clone it. When Mark Zuckerberg launched Facebook, he ran a campaign targeted at Harvard students. Once he had 50 percent of the undergraduate students on Facebook, he repeated the same process at Stanford, then Columbia, then Yale. Facebook has unlimited supply—that's the beauty of cloud computing. Zuckerberg's mission from the outset was to clone his demand generators.

The McDonald's franchise is a good example of a cloning strategy that bundles supply and demand into one package. When McDonald's opens a new outlet, it's a cloning exercise. The new outlet is almost identical to the previous one, and on the day of opening, there is brand-new supply (kitchen, staff, tables) as well as new demand (the local community).

Cloning comes in different shapes and sizes.

Perfect Cloning vs. Imperfect Cloning

An assembly line of cars is perfect cloning since each car is a replica of the previous one. But few things are perfect. Think of it as a sliding scale.

The construction of an architect-designed house is an example of imperfect cloning. The builder must work hard to figure out ways to turn the architect's drawings into reality. The project may be similar to the previous one, but it will also be different. A predesigned project home is also imperfect cloning due to the unique challenges of a building location; however, it does lean to the side of perfect cloning.

Temporary Clones vs. Permanent Clones

This is also a sliding scale. A car is a temporary clone in the sense that the business benefits from it only temporarily. For example, a Tesla car gets shipped to the customer, the money is received, and the profit goes into this quarter's statements. That's it. The car now becomes irrelevant to Tesla. Well, it's still relevant in the sense that it's an advertisement on wheels and Tesla needs to honor the warranty, but you get the point. The car is not helping Tesla to increase its production capacity. The Tesla car is temporary.

A new assembly line, on the other hand, is a more permanent clone and helps greatly to increase production capacity.

The ideal is obviously to have cloning processes in place that are perfect and permanent, covering both supply and demand. This combination is worth billions. But since these are sliding scales, we don't have to aim for perfection. Simply see if you can move the dial closer to perfection and closer to permanence for both the demand side and supply side.

So how does this apply to tech services?

There are basically two types of cloning that happen naturally:

1. Hire more consultants, and put each new consultant through the same onboarding process in the hope that they will fit in.

2. Win new projects in the hope that each new project will be similar to the previous one.

But these two cloning strategies don't take us very far. Eventually, we reach a saturation point. And this is because both mechanisms are imperfect and quite temporary. A consultant might stay for five years; a project might last one year; a support engagement might last three years. For every project that ends, we need to win a new one just to stay in business.

The situation can be improved drastically by keeping your staff longer, by selling long-term engagements, by sticking to your niche, and by delivering projects that are near-perfect clones of each other. I'm effectively arguing that you should turn down more consultants and turn down more work. How exactly will this help you grow? To grow sustainably, you need to change the game.

Changing the Game

Think in terms of higher-order cloning, as in multiple assembly lines. Become an expert at launching new practices, new teams, new regions, new offerings, etc. without compromising your reputation as a niche player.

Bluleader was a single-region business that expanded by cloning practices. First, there was an SAP CRM on-premise practice, then an SAP CRM in the cloud practice, then an e-commerce practice, then a digital practice, and finally, a Microsoft Dynamics practice. All these practices were true to the niche since they all related to customer experience.

Presence of IT, a leading consultancy and provider of the world's foremost human capital management solutions, grew to a client base of more than 600 consultants serving their own clients in multiple industries across the world by cloning its SAP HCM practice into an Oracle HCM practice. They then went global by opening offices in multiple countries.[41]

On the other hand, if you venture into a new region with a new offering and hire new staff to run the show, you have expanded. However, you haven't cloned anything because, if you've changed that much in your business all at the same time, you've created something brand new rather than changed something small to keep you on the same path. This is an expansion strategy rather than a cloning strategy, and such an expansion has a lower chance of success.

So, if you move into a new region, do it with a current staff member and a current offering, and focus on the act of cloning. This way, out of the three factors (region, offering, staff), only one is new, and the act of cloning can now be focused on one thing only: getting the region up and running.

If you move into a new offering (e.g., start a new practice), ideally do it in your main region where the new practice manager can learn the ropes from other practice managers. In this situation, too, be sure to do it with existing staff.

There are cases where it may be better to find an expert from outside the business to launch the new practice and gain instant recognition (due to their reputation). This unfortunately means that out of the three factors (region, offering, staff), two are new. This process will be more painful but totally worth it if the new manager receives strong support. We found this at Bluleader, when we brought in an outside person well known in the industry to run a new practice for us. By giving him much support, that practice grew to be highly successful.

So, as you can see, the setup and execution of your "always-on" engines is critical for your growth. So how do we keep these engines going, utilizing finite and, potentially, limited resources? We do it using a strategy known as "scaffolding."

Key Takeaways

1. Always think of ways to reuse and repurpose what has been built on projects, and turn these into accelerators for the future.

2. Use automation wherever you can to drive efficiency.

3. Ensure that you have healthy meeting rhythms across the business to keep a strong focus on the measures and objectives of the business.

4. Work out your economic denominator that will allow you to scale using cloning.

CHAPTER 18

The Scaffolding Approach

You might look at all the activities required to keep all eight engines running and wonder how on earth you will achieve this, especially in the earlier phases of the business when there are not many of you. This is exactly where I was at Bluleader. The way we dealt with the challenge was via the technique of scaffolding. This approach recognizes that you cannot afford to recruit someone to own and run each of these engines when you are smaller; therefore, you create a "scaffold" to run them.

The concept comes from Keith McFarland's book *The Breakthrough Company*, which used a research study of nine businesses that broke through to become successful companies after some time of stagnation. McFarland found that each breakthrough company was surrounded by a network of outside resources vital to their success.

"We call these resources 'scaffolding' because, like physical scaffolding, they are *temporary structures that exist outside the organization itself and enable the company to get to the next level.*"[37]

For example, for demand and lead generation, you might contract a copywriter for four hours a week to edit and curate "rough" content the staff has produced rather than hiring a marketing manager and building a marketing team. You could also, for example, contract a senior project manager for a short period of time to create a project delivery framework and templates based on that intellectual property rather than hiring a delivery manager and forming a project management office (PMO).

Bringing in outside experts to assist you in getting your engines up and running—a marketing consultant, a recruitment firm, a bookkeeping assistant—is easier in the post-pandemic world, as so many people are able to operate virtually. This fosters an excellent environment to scaffold your engines. You could even consider individuals from your customer base or your vendors to serve in these roles.

To articulate this in a real-life case study, I have been working with a client whom I've finally convinced to run aggressive marketing with razor-sharp focus. This client is an all-or-nothing kind of guy, and he believed he needed to hire a full-time marketing expert to his staff to create an aggressive marketing campaign. However, he's not making nearly enough money to justify it just yet. Right now, he just needs someone who can come in and help one day a week—a freelancer who can operate at an hourly rate.

Note that your goal here is to get the engines up and running rather than delaying any further. This is your scaffold. The engines may be tiny at first, but at least they're in motion. Your scaffold sits around your engines and provides structure and stability while you're busy building. Eventually, as the business begins to make more money through healthy and "always-on" demand-generation, lead-generation, and sales engines, you will hire full-time staff to further support those engines and fully own the execution as a mastermind.

The end goal is that the building will be able to stand on its own—your engines will be "always on," meaning they now run without your direct, hands-on involvement.

You have to control your dollars to drive growth, and it's a fine balance. If you don't, you'll either end up bankrupt in six months because you spent too much money, or you'll be in the same place as you started because you did not take action.

Big vs. Small

I understand that you may be reading this book because you have a large company that has hit a ceiling that you can't seem to break through in terms of growth and scale. Therefore, you may be asking if scaffolding is necessary in your situation. In short, when you are a large company, you don't need it. You can have everything in-house.

On the other hand, if your company operates with fewer than 100 employees, you probably need scaffolding around at least one, if not a few, of the engines. As a smaller business, you likely can't afford to hire and assign full-time staff to every engine. Eventually, each engine will have a team of people who will take care of that engine. But you don't have the money for that right now.

Large companies will have a marketing team responsible for demand generation. They're paid employees with a set budget. So, if you're a large company, you employ people, and you give KPIs, the big question is "How will you get all these engines to work optimally?" The answer comes down to planning and execution, which we'll lay out in the sections that follow.

When you have a small company, you scaffold. You pay someone offshore to do outbound calling to start generating leads. You add a weekly responsibility to one of your practice leads to stay on-site one day a week to focus solely on sales rather than going to clients. You tie KPIs to those functions, and once you start growing, you add a full-time sales position (that same practice manager may transition into that role if they enjoy it). Then, as you grow, you'll have a team and a manager already in place.

One final approach is automation. Keep in mind, though, that if you're planning to hire external people for tasks that could be automated, you're wasting money. Marketing systems can send automated emails, for example. The Catch-22 is that people use the excuse of "I don't have time to set up automation, so I'll just do it manually myself." All you need is a few days to set up a system and then you can move on to more important things. Small or large, if you're not automating, you're wasting time, resources, and most importantly, money that could be used to take down the scaffolding and reinforce the structure and foundation of the building.

Define Your Engines

Create space in your A3 Strategy to define each engine and what it means for your business. You should also encapsulate the vision for each engine in a clear, specific paragraph.

It's important to note that not all of the engines will be at the same level of maturity at different stages of the business and particularly not at the exit. Therefore, your vision for each engine will differ by business strategy and targeted exit, e.g., if your target exit trigger is a $5 million business with 20 people, the people engine might consist of a single, part-time recruiter. However, a business targeting $50 million might have a human resources manager with a dedicated recruiter and part-time people administrator.

Use the table below to understand your level of maturity in each of your engines. For each of the engine categories listed in the first column, give your business a rating according to the numbers in the header row across the top.

ENGINE MATURITY LEVELS

Rating	0->1	1->2	2->3	3>4	>4
Maturity Level	Manual	Bursts	Long runs with pauses	Always-on	Always-on and optimized
Mastermind	Tactical	Emergent strategy	Strategy drives the portfolio	Dominant market position	Visionary and agile
Demand	Ad-hoc market comms	Flurry of communication to the market	Planned demand plan in execution	Stream of constant communications	Constant stream of multi-channel communications that are being consumed by target audience
Lead	Reactive	Campaign-driven	Programmatic	Strategic	Industry-leading
Sales	Tactical	Busy when there are many leads; reactive	Opportunity management is managed across the team, pauses when delivery is busy	Strong account planning; pipeline planning	Detailed account planning; high bid–win ratio; accurate sales forecasts
Production	Varies across projects; methods put together as work arises	Standard methods	Methods, tools, IP across the the business	Resource management;, PMO	Collaborative with advanced systems
Back Office	No plan/budget; no systems or metrics	Budget and metrics in place	Budget and metrics using integrated systems	Real-time metrics and self service	Real-time forward- and backward-looking analysis with insights
People	Reactive	Project based; team events held to address issues e.g., low morale, fatigue	Recruitment plan; pipeline being established; sporadic team events	Recruitment pipeline in place; good onboarding process; culture being established	Clear recruitment pipeline aligned with sales forecast; strong company culture; sought-after place to work
Scale	Scale metrics unknown; roles undefined	Planning of profit centers happening; rough idea of scope and metrics	One profit center established with measures; others being planned	Profit centers established and being measured; clear roles established; future plans not yet formulated	Clear scale metrics; clear role definitions; financial plan in place

In terms of driving maturity of these engines, some will seem more critical than others at different times. Stephen Covey's Urgent Important Matrix is a great way to remember that some of the engines, like sales and production, will always generate a higher sense of immediacy and urgency. Other engines, like demand, are longer term and therefore can be neglected. So, always ensure that your business is applying the correct amount of effort and thinking to all engines.[38]

URGENT-IMPORTANT MATRIX

Once you have completed all of the above assessments, you can produce a maturity radar chart like the one below.

ENGINE MATURITY SPIDER DIAGRAM

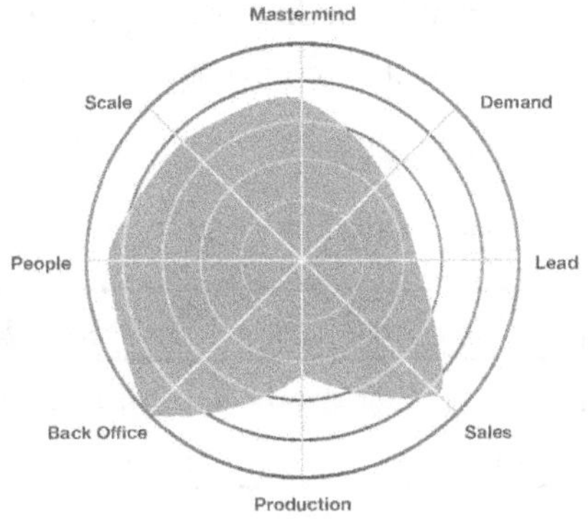

This chart can also be visualized as a set of control room gauges:

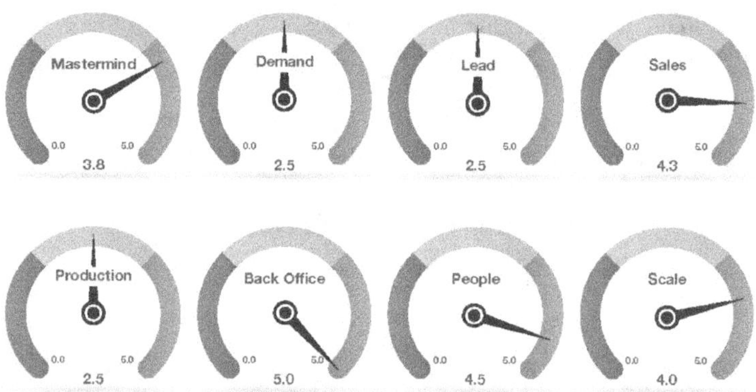

Lagging and Leading Indicators

Many people confuse lag and lead indicators and end up drawing false conclusions. For example, you might look at a financial report and see that profits have consistently grown over the last three years and therefore conclude that profits will continue in that vein. What is clear here is that looking at previous profits is a lag indicator, albeit an important one. It is therefore critical to know what your lead indicators are because they are the predictors of where you are going and whether or not you are on track. Lead indicators are things like future coverage, opportunity pipeline, or projected costs.

The lead and lag indicators for the engines are shown below:

Engine	Lead	Lag
Mastermind	Clear mastermind defined	Nimble and rapid decision-making

Engine	Lead	Lag
Demand	Amount of content pieces created; social following; webinar volume; quantity of referenceable customers	Market awareness of your company
Lead	Volume of client interactions (outbound)	Quantity of inbound leads
Sales	Total number of active clients; length of sales cycle; pipeline coverage (opportunities forecast); sales margin	Bid-to-win ratio; closed deals size; revenue growth; business profitability
Production	Percentage of projects using a standard delivery method; effectiveness of resource management; estimating effectiveness	Billable utilization; on-time project delivery; percentage of project overrun; revenue per consultant; percentage of project margin
Back Office	Backlog; month-end close duration	DSO; percentage of revenue leakage; percentage of targets achieved; percentage of redone invoices

Engine	Lead	Lag
People	Great place to work rating; training days per person; clear career path	Attrition rate
Scale	Defined denominator; clear niche	Time from practice inception to profitability

Use this chart as a guide as you build the scaffolding around your engines. Not all of these will apply to your business right now, so be sure to only use those that are true leads and lags in your situation.

All these exercises are mandatory steps toward building that foundation. Use them to understand the resources you need to ensure your engines are "always on."

Meeting Rhythm

The key to succeeding is to have one individual running each of your engines to whom you provide weekly direction, expectations, and KPIs. Each week, you also check up on what should have been done the week prior and that you are still on track to accomplishing your daily, weekly, monthly, and quarterly goals. It cascades from there.

To ensure that each engine maintains its momentum, it should follow its own meeting rhythm, which can be a powerful cadence to meet your business's growth needs.

For many, there is a belief that if you are small, then meetings are overkill. Meetings are for big companies, right? This is not true by any measure and was a big learning experience for us. One of the most impactful books on this topic is Patrick Lencioni's *Death by Meeting*. Once you understand how a meeting rhythm connects with the tasks, goals, and anchors within your business, you'll begin to see consistent momentum building.

It's important to understand that not all meetings have the same purpose. Meetings can become very ineffective when their intended purposes are diluted across numerous meetings. Lencioni uses the analogy of the television show. He explains that if we mixed a news highlight program with a three-hour film or a 10-part drama series, the result would be greatly underwhelming.[39] Meetings should be viewed in the same way.

The meeting objective or purpose is within a continuum of highly tactical (dealing with day-to-day issues) right up to highly strategic (focusing on long-term objectives). The more tactical a meeting, the more frequently it should be held.

Meeting Frequencies

Here's a meeting rhythm we created for our business:

Daily. A tactical meeting that focuses on tasks to be performed within the day. The best example is the daily stand-up meeting, which should be held with a leader and his team. It should run for no longer than 15 minutes without a preset agenda of topics other than for each team member to explain briefly what they are doing that day, any blockers they may have, or assistance they need. This meeting is not designed to resolve issues but rather to identify them so that a separate smaller group can look at resolutions. As this is a meeting looking at the day ahead, hold it at the beginning of the day.

Weekly. *This* is still a tactical meeting but focused on activities that run over multiple days. These meetings will not have fixed agenda topics but will follow a framework. The most typical example is the sales meeting. (Others are recruitment, marketing, or back-office team meetings.) A sales meeting will run for one to two hours, depending on the size of the sales team. It will include those with a direct impact on a sales outcome. The team will review and discuss current leads and opportunities, once again homing in on blockers. There is a tendency in weekly meetings to want to discuss strategic items; however, this is not the forum for it. If major points do arise, park them for discussion at the monthly strategy meeting.

Monthly. *A* strategic meeting where tactical day-to-day issues must be left at the door. Significant strategic issues that have come up in the month should be discussed here. Typically, this meeting should run for two to four hours (with no time limit set) and focus on two to three large, strategic topics—the idea being that the meeting does not conclude until actions and plans have been created around these topics.

Quarterly. *The* quarterly off-site meeting is by far the most strategic meeting you will have within the business (other than the board meeting). Its purpose is to set strategic targets for the next quarter. The outputs from this off-site meeting are an updated set of anchors—entered into the A3 Strategy for the next quarter—as well as resulting subactions for all team members.

The Engines and Meeting Rhythm

The meeting rhythm serves two very important purposes: keeping the A3 Strategy on track and maintaining the engines.

To ensure that the engines are optimized, those within the engine should follow the same meeting rhythm for their teams. For example, the people engine team should have a daily stand-up, a weekly tactical meeting, and a monthly strategic meeting. Depending on the size of the business, the engine team members can either join a combined quarterly strategic meeting or have their own. The important point here is that the engines must maintain constant momentum and focus on their goals just like the overall business.

Board Meetings

Depending on the structure of your business (considering things like its current size and number of directors), you will want to have a monthly or quarterly board meeting. Clearly, items to be discussed here should be concerned with business performance, governance, and compliance, as well as strategic topics that impact the shareholders. Many smaller businesses do not see the need for a board meeting, rather preferring to discuss these items informally. At Bluleader, we found the board meeting to be extremely important when we had nonexecutive directors and multiple shareholders. Key items to be resolved at these sessions are

- bringing on new shareholders,

- seeking business investments,

- business expansions into other regions, and

- executive leadership team appointments and structures.

Yearly, Quarterly, and Monthly Goals

The concept of the A3 Strategy, the MATE Framework, and the Sweat2Scale approach is really one of setting your long-term targets and breaking them down into smaller and smaller tasks. For example, if you want to have a staff of 100 within five years, work backward with logic as follows:

Year 5: 100 people = 33% growth

Year 4: 75 people = 50% growth

Year 3: 50 people = 100% growth

Year 2: 25 people = 150% growth

Year 1: 10 people

By doing this, the 100 people target is less daunting, especially if you then break down year one into quarterly goals. However, you don't just want goals because those can quickly turn into aspirations, or something that may happen someday. You want them to be predictions. In other words, what we *will* achieve (not what we *hope* to achieve).

These anchors must be defined every quarter. They are the sub-tasks that allow you to achieve your annual priorities. I recommend that you and your leadership team define these in a quarterly off-site meeting. Quarterly meetings are necessary because as the business grows, your goals will need to be dynamic and reflect the context of the business at any point in time.

The anchors must have deadlines and owners allocated to them. Anchor tracking should be carried out every week in a tactical team meeting. They should be front of mind throughout the quarter as they are what will move you toward your BHAG. The minimum number of anchors should be three per quarter. When you are smaller, that should be more than sufficient.

This all equates to setting SMART goals. These anchors should be Simple, Measurable, Attainable, Realistic, and Timely, and if you can't get them completed in the time you set for them, they should be broken down further.

From there, you'd break down your quarterly goals into monthly goals. Your individual engine masterminds then take those and break them down into weekly and daily to-do activities, to which you should make yourself accountable. If you set all of that up, it's a near guarantee that you will achieve your goals.

Now we will dive into some deeper, more technical strategies to scale even further. In the next chapter, we'll look at some of these execution factors that will take you to the next level and move you closer to your end goal or exit strategy.

Key Takeaways

1. Scaffolding means creating a temporary structure using people from outside the organization to enable the company to get to the next level.

2. Large companies may not need scaffolding, but small companies operating with fewer than 100 employees likely need it in at least one of the engines.

3. Look at using scaffolding, the right leaders, regular meetings, constant lead-indicator measures, and automation within each engine to ensure they are *all* "always on."

CHAPTER 19

For Smaller Companies: Focus on Revenue Streams, Intellectual Property, and Barriers to Revenue

Now that you have all your engines set up and "always on," and you have a road map (via the A3 Strategy) for how you will grow and scale in the next one to five years, you are ready to execute in even more granular ways.

As a tech services firm, what types of revenue should you focus on?

What are some of the barriers that smaller firms face? Is there any value to having intellectual property (IP)?

Types of Revenue

There are a number of sources and types of revenue within a technology services business, as outlined in the examples in the table below.

TYPES OF TECH SERVICES REVENUE

Revenue Type	Characteristics	Pros	Cons	When to Use
Time and Materials	Most common for services businesses. Customer pays for time and costs expended.	Low risk. Simple to administer. Predictable forecasting. Likelihood of losing money is low	Time can only be sold once. Difficult to recover "lost" time.	Best option for work that is unpredictable or difficult to estimate. Easiest for smaller businesses that do not have strong project management.
Fixed Price	Projects or components of work are charged as a fixed price irrespective of actual time or cost to deliver.	Potential for high margins. Can make your offering very competitive	Higher risk. Difficult to administer. Can create an "us and them" culture between the customer and supplier	When the work being delivered is well understood and scoped. When you have strong project management in place.

Revenue Type	Characteristics	Pros	Cons	When to Use
Shared Risk	Risk is shared with a customer. There is typically a fixed-price component and a shared upside/downside creating a situation where you and the customer have aligned financial interests.	Aligns the customer and vendor, if managed well. Lowers risk of loss	Difficult to administer and financially plan. Will not work with every client's organizational culture	When the customer has a partnership culture and wants to work collaboratively to manage budget. Requires strong project management from supplier and customer, as well as a well-functioning and empowered steering committee.
Managed Services	Long-term contract with a customer to deliver a fixed set of services within a committed service level	Predictable revenue stream. Creates customer "stickiness". Can be very profitable if using cost-effective resourcing models	Challenging to resource when there is no scale. Can be low margin if using the same resources as project delivery. Money can be lost if SLAs are not met	With highly repeatable activities and lower-cost resource models

Revenue Type	Characteristics	Pros	Cons	When to Use
Retainer	A fixed fee paid on a periodic basis (e.g., monthly) for a fixed period to provide a certain quantity of time or services. The services are typically broader than managed services.	Predictable revenue stream. Creates customer "stickiness" leading to the creation of other revenue (if transferred out of the scope of the retainer)	Can be difficult to manage scope if retainer is not well defined. Can be difficult to resource if work scope is too broad	When the type of work varies over time, but the client is looking for vendor/ resource continuity
Resale	Reselling of software for a software vendor. Your business is remunerated by adding a margin or receiving an incentive from the vendor.	Increases margin on service projects. Creates "stickiness" with the customer. Creates deeper working approach with the vendor, potentially leading to more leads	Diminishes some of the "independent advisor" status you may have. Not the same as selling services, therefore requires different approaches and people for the sales process	When the product is squarely in your niche and will be seen as a "value-add" by the customer. Should not ever detract from the core business, i.e., service delivery.

Barriers to Entry and How to Overcome Them

There are numerous barriers to entry for smaller firms that make it difficult for you to win work or even bid for work with certain clients. In the early days of your business, a key focus will be to win larger deals in your own right. To achieve this, you should follow the crawl-walk-run approach.

Start off by placing yourself and your staff at client sites either directly or via a larger system integrator—the crawl phase. Your focus here is to win revenue as well as create a base of reference for your business. So, it's critical that your business name is known even if it means placing single individuals on a larger project. Negotiate up front with the larger SI or end customer to get a reference or a case study for pieces of work you have done. This is crucial for the next phase.

In the walk phase, the goal is to win a smaller deal that is "primed" (you are the prime contractor) by your business. To do this, you will need references (as mentioned before), a strong methodology, and strong staff members well respected by the prospective client. Once again, negotiate references with your client up front.

To move into the run phase, winning larger deals in your own right, you will need strong references from the previous phases. The barriers to these larger deals now come into play:

Government Panels

If the public sector is a target market for your business, invariably, you will need to ensure that you are on the correct government procurement panels. Depending on the jurisdiction, there could be many hurdles to jump to get onto these panels. There really is no secret other than to go through the process methodically. Early on, while still in the crawl phase, you should determine what requirements you need to meet. Once you know these, you can start to build toward meeting them.

For example, if one requirement is a customer case study on demonstrated capability, then make sure you start early and build a bank of these. Don't wait until you are actually submitting a panel tender. Another approach is to engage in this public sector work via a third party that is on the panel. This will allow you to build references within these public sector businesses. Be aware, however, that although this will give you relevant industry references, it could preclude you from later working directly with the particular client.

Private Panels

Some large private sector clients have approved procurement panels too. The same concepts and approaches mentioned for government panels apply. Another key ingredient to achieving entry onto any panel is the niche focus. If you are the undisputed experts in a particular niche, companies will make a way to get you onto the panels. The more generalist you are, the more competition and worse off you will look on paper.

Scale Perception Preventing Entry into Large Customers or Deals

In many cases, the perception of your company size will be a hindrance to being allowed to bid on certain larger pieces of work. To overcome this, once again, being the leader and known as such in your particular niche is essential. Partnering with larger partners or creating a consortium with other similar-size businesses is an alternative method to addressing this scale objection.

How to Approach IP

To drive higher margins and more sustainable revenue, tech services businesses look for alternative approaches and efficiencies.

Product Development

Many in the tech services business have a rose-colored view when it comes to product development. They believe life would be so much easier if only they had a product they could sell, as it would allow for easier scaling. That is the allure of products for companies that sell time. The reality is that developing products is a very different skill set to running a services business, and many of these companies fail at ever deriving a large percentage of their revenue from products.

There is also a massive underestimation of the time and money needed to develop enterprise-grade solutions. The often-forgotten piece of the puzzle is the ongoing infrastructure and teams to support and maintain solutions that have been sold. All this does not mean you should not pursue product development, but I would recommend you do extensive research on what is required to carry it out. A well-costed business plan should be in place to understand what the cash flow will look like—hire a specialist in software development to run this initiative. Another possibility to explore is to co-develop a software solution with a customer, therefore sharing the risk and cost as well as testing the solution in a real-life situation.

Accelerators

These are good alternatives to full product development within tech services businesses. Accelerators are components that quickly advance the delivery of projects, thereby lowering risk (due to repeatability), increasing margin (if these parts are built in as fixed-price components), or making you more competitive (costing less than your competitors).

Accelerators can be developed over time through projects with customers. Many customers, by default, insist in their contracts that all IP developed on their systems is to be owned by them, so clear IP ownership should be negotiated up front with a view to ensuring mutual benefit (discounting for them) and undertakings regarding use by competitors. If customers do not agree to release IP, you will need to develop solutions within your own systems environment and with your own allocated funds, i.e., not leveraging what you developed for the customer. I believe accelerators are definitely worth creating within your technology services business—as opposed to product development.

Own Methodology

In very much the same vein as accelerators, having your own methodology with templates, checklists, and how-to guides will be invaluable in driving consistent quality of delivery and, therefore, the ability to scale. This is a challenging area, as it falls into the category of "important" but not "urgent." If it's left simply to happen without a plan and allocated budget, it tends to never happen. To ensure it does, take two steps:

- Have a KPI for some key staff to create parts or all of this methodology; in particular, the checklists and how-to guides.

- Bring in an external expert on a contract and have a budget allocated to a methodology-creation project.

Create a culture of "harvesting" learnings from projects using KPIs, and structure team playbacks that enforce a deadline for delivery.

The final factor in effective execution is all about holding everyone accountable to your commitment to carry out all the elements of your A3 Strategy. In the next chapter, I offer tips and measures to put into place from top to bottom.

Key Takeaways

1. There are numerous types of revenue, each with its own characteristics, pros, and cons.

2. Understand your barriers to entry and work on a crawl-walk-run approach to breaking through these.

3. Generate appropriate intellectual property for your business.

CHAPTER 20

Multidimensional Accountability

By now, you know the importance of getting out of the way and allowing your eight "always-on" engines to run without getting your hands too dirty. To do this, you must hold your teams owning those engines accountable. In chapter 18, we discussed the engines in detail as well as the importance of establishing a meeting rhythm. A meeting is the framework on which you hold your teams accountable.

The whole idea behind the scaffolding approach is that you assign someone to work on a specific engine and that you meet with that individual (or individuals) once per week. It's imperative that you show up to that meeting and give direction, but do not do tasks for your engines yourself every week. Your role is to keep them up and running while you focus on the bigger picture—all the right things to grow and scale the business.

Millionaire Mentor told me a story about a newcomer to his business who was a highly reputable salesperson. After a few weeks at the company, he asked why they weren't holding weekly sales meetings. He convinced the ownership group that these were critical because they had to hold him accountable. He wanted a framework on which they could relay their expectations to him, and he could come back to the next meeting and tell them he'd met those expectations.

So, at Bluleader, I insisted we run sales meetings. The moral of the story is that people who are high performers should ask you to hold them accountable. When you have people who don't want to be held accountable, you may have a problem, and if you have that problem, you won't get results. Accountability doesn't just benefit one salesperson. It benefits your entire sales team.

Establishing expectations was an area in which I struggled during the early days at Bluleader. My greatest challenge was my mindset—I treated employees as if they operated exactly like me. However, the reality was that I never set proper expectations of their responsibilities. I frequently thought to myself, "They're going off the rails and doing what they want," but the problem was, I hadn't actually told them what to do.

The most effective way to communicate to employees or project owners what you want them to do is to have clear KPIs that are not super complicated. You don't need 10 different things on the weekly task list. Narrow those down to five goals, and be sure to communicate what they are and how you will measure them. Then, use your weekly meeting to track how those goals are trending toward those measurable outcomes and give real-time feedback. You shouldn't have to micromanage if you hire the right people. They will know what to do to meet your KPIs.

Another lesson I learned was that instead of holding my teams accountable to course correcting when things went off the rails, I was helping them fix the situation. This is a common problem with entrepreneurs—especially those who were once on the tools and now are running a business. In the tech services world, you have technologists who have mostly dealt with others in a similar trade who speak the same language. When they get off the tools and start running a business, they are exposed to working with other teams who speak in completely different business terms.

Create an organizational accountability framework within the business like the one below, which defines the organization's functions and roles. Then list leading indicator metrics for each function and measure them weekly in a scorecard. This will ensure that everyone in the organization is clear on their roles and what is expected of them. People respond positively when they know their expectations and whether or not they are on track.

ROLES AND MEASURES

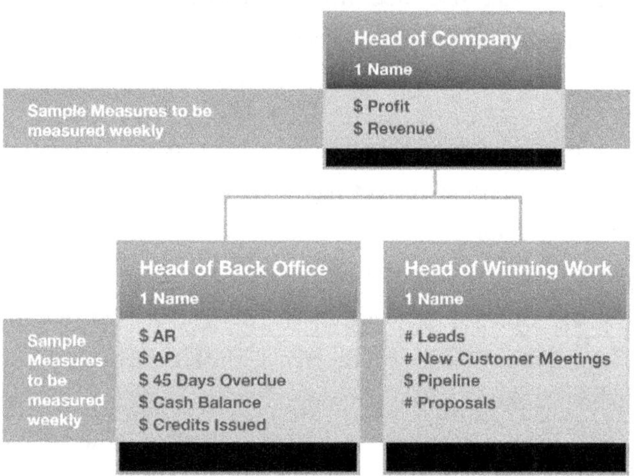

Another trap to avoid is alienating accountability in favor of being "a cool company." Millionaire Mentor told me that originally, he wanted to run a cool company with cool bosses and cool employees. They didn't give people KPIs, because that's not cool. Needless to say, that approach backfired. They ended up with people who didn't know their roles—who didn't have clear expectations. That's not cool. It's much akin to raising children. Giving kids boundaries on knowing what they are supposed to do and what not to do creates a stable and safe space. It's much worse when they don't have boundaries because they don't know what the limits are, and then they begin to act out. Employees are the same (perhaps to a lesser extent) because without clear expectations, measurable goals, and rapid feedback, they will never know if they're doing their jobs properly.

David Shein said on a webinar with the Sweat2Scale team, "Someone asked me recently, 'Can you be an empathetic leader, a caring leader, but also demand high performance?' To me, the two go hand-in-hand because you can't do amazing things for your staff without high performance. You can't send them on training courses. You can't pay bonuses. You can't do so many things if you are not delivering results. So yes, both are, in my opinion, absolutely interrelated."[42]

Reid Hoffman, the founder of LinkedIn, argues in a *Harvard Business Review* article that your company is not a family; rather, a company is more like a sports team. And the leaders of the company are like the coach who really cares for the players, but the players also have to perform, and if they perform, they enjoy it.[43]

One final story to drive these points home: In the third year at Millionaire Mentor's company, they noticed a lot of consultants would just come to the office whenever they felt like it and would randomly not be available to do billable work for a customer for the day. The owners thought, "That's weird. Why would they do that?" After Millionaire Mentor talked to them about the situation, those consultants said they'd just go back to the customer the next day. Shortly afterward, the ownership group announced they'd give the consultants a KPI of how many billable days they'd be responsible for per year.

One of the star consultants asked, "Is this what you always wanted?" When Millionaire Mentor replied, "Yes," the consultant responded, "Why didn't you tell us?"

His first thought was "Because it's obvious!" However, it wasn't obvious to the consultants. So, from there, not only did Millionaire Mentor give them KPIs, but he also gave them a bonus if they could do more than 200 billable days per year. He even started highlighting the biggest billers in the company, and it paid off big time. Yet, for a while there, the ownership group had just assumed everyone knew they needed to be very billable. Once they made the employees aware that they were watching, tracking, and incentivizing, productivity increased well beyond satisfaction.

A Quick Note on Shareholder Accountability

Aside from your employees, when you are part of an ownership group, you also have to keep each other in check. The key here is to execute this practice without attacking one another in front of your employees. As the business ramps up, tensions may be high. As we've stated before, it is important to face these demons and nip them in the bud before it's too late. (We discussed this in chapter 13.) I also recommend enlisting an unbiased third party if you can't come to a quick resolution. Once the owners are on the same page, this harmony should trickle down to the employees. When there's turmoil at the top, what do you think happens down below?

The Final, Most Important Form of Accountability

Even the greatest businessperson will tell you, "If I've read all of this and don't actually do anything, I've failed." You can see this attitude in great sports teams and businesses alike. When you have someone holding the owner, general manager, CEO, or whoever is at the top accountable, that's when you achieve greatness.

Business owners become extremely busy doing all the urgent stuff, and a lot of them intuitively know what they need to do. They have goals, but because they're the owners, they're accountable to no one other than themselves—especially if they are single business owners and not a part of an ownership group. However, even if you are a part of an ownership group, you may find yourself floundering.

At Bluleader, I had all these things to do, but I was not accountable to anyone in my business. There was no one to tell me that I hadn't done the most important task at hand until Millionaire Mentor came along as an external advisor and asked the tough questions. When he started to hold me accountable and regularly ask if I'd been making progress toward my goals, I really started seeing more rapid change in my company. I never wanted to go back to him and say, "No, I haven't done it yet."

A third-party advisor or consultant works great for people who own businesses, because they give you external validation. Some, especially narcissistic personality types don't want to be held accountable—they don't like to be told that they're not meeting their objectives. But most people like hearing "Well done, you've done it!" and respond well.

Therefore, I highly recommend enlisting a business advisor, a personal accountability coach, or a scaling and growth consultant to propel your progress forward at higher speeds. The service is truly worth its weight in gold.

Key Takeaways

1. People who are high performers should ask to be held accountable, and those who don't want to be held accountable may be problematic.

2. You should not have to micromanage if you hire the right people.

3. Avoid the trap of helping teams fix situations rather than holding them accountable to course correct when things go off the rails. Provide rapid feedback and avoid alienating accountability because you want to be "a cool company."

4. Empathy and high performance go hand-in-hand.

5. Your company is more like a sports team than a family, and the leaders of the company are like the coaches who care for the players but also must perform in their own right.

CHAPTER 21

House of Cards

Throughout the journey of building Bluleader, there came moments where it felt as if things were about to implode. It felt, at many times, like a house of cards.

From the outside, it all looked great, but inside, there was frantic pedaling. These moments occurred when there was a crisis with a customer, such as a project not going well, a conflict within the team, or a market challenge—such as a global financial crisis!

It's important to know that these feelings are totally normal, and further, I suggest it's what ensures your business's success as it shows you don't take anything for granted. It's quite common to hear other business owners making statements like "This thing (*the business*) feels crazy, like it could collapse any time but is doing really well," or, "We're hiring so many people, we have the work, but what happens if it dries up? How will we feed all these mouths?" or, "Everyone sees us doing so well … if they only knew what it was like on the inside!"

There are several techniques I learned and applied over the years to get through these times. Here are the most pertinent:

Improve on the Worst Case

When Millionaire Mentor first joined Bluleader, he recommended I read an old book that is still highly relevant today, *How to Stop Worrying and Start Living* by Dale Carnegie. There were two concepts that stood out to me, which I applied over and over. Firstly, in a crisis, understand what the absolute worst-case outcome could be, assess whether you could live with that outcome, and then work hard to do better than the worst case. This mindset shift radically reduces stress levels and allows much better thinking and focus on solving the problem.[44]

Day-Tight Compartments or "Put the Glass Down"

A second technique that Carnegie spoke about was the concept of day-tight compartments—the analogy being that of a ship having watertight compartments that will seal in case of a leak, therefore preventing water from flowing from compartment to compartment. The idea here, particularly for a tech services business, which has many problems to deal with every day—is that you can only focus on today and do it really well. This is the best preparation for the future.[45]

Take going into the weekend as an example: don't take Monday's problems with you. Resolve them on Monday. This technique takes practice but can dramatically reduce worry and stress. It is not advocating for ignoring the future but rather only focusing on items that need to be done today that are needed for today or that might have future impact. It's also important to not dwell on the past. The past is purely used to apply learnings to today. Every day is a new life to a wise person.

To simplify the concept, consider this parable:

A professor enters his classroom with a glass of water. He raises the glass of water. The professor smiles and inquires, "How heavy is this glass of water?" The students call answers in the range of 200 grams to 400 grams. He replies, "I need to weigh it to know exactly how much it weighs. But the question I really want you to answer is, 'What if I held the glass up for a minute?'"

The students answer unanimously, "Nothing."

"But what if I held it up for an hour?" the professor asks.

"Your arms will start aching," answers a student.

"You're right! But what if I held it up for a whole day?" he asks.

"Your arms will feel numb, your muscles will get stressed, and they may even become paralyzed," volunteers another student.

"Correct!" remarks the professor. "So, what should I do to avoid the pain?" he asks.

"Put the glass down," answers a student.

"Precisely!" says the professor. He continues, "In all cases, the weight of the glass remains the same. The longer it is up, the heavier it becomes. The stress and worries in life are like the glass of water. If you think

about them for a while, nothing happens. Think about them for longer, they will start hurting. Think about them for even longer, you will feel stress and become paralyzed."

The Doctor

A mindset I had to adopt while scaling Bluleader was accepting that as the business grew, my role would increasingly become one of a problem-solver or escalation point. I would move away from a lot of the "doing" and become much more of the collection point for business challenges that need solving.

Rather than seeing this as a negative, I had to learn to look at it as a sign of business growth. The analogy I was given was one of a doctor. A doctor's role, all that they study for, is to listen to people's problems and to provide solutions. If a doctor complained about this, it would not make any sense, as this is precisely the role they had worked so hard to assume. In the same way, the more your business grows, the larger the problems are that need solving. This is, in fact, an achievement! To quote Uncle Ben from *Spider-Man*, "With great power comes great responsibility."

Be Ready to Scale Down

Technology services businesses can be affected quite dramatically by external forces, such as rapid client spend, the loss of a vendor, or general direction changes. This is especially true if the revenue spread is not well diversified (defined as having any single client who generates more than 20 to 25 percent of total revenue). In the earlier stages of a company, this nonoptimal revenue spread can happen quite easily.

At Bluleader, this occurred a few times as we pushed to grow the business and won larger deals. Some of these larger deals, which were game-changers for us, did grow the business rapidly. The drawback was that they could have potentially exposed the business to risk if these clients rapidly reduced spend. This was the case with one large customer, who rapidly cut spending from one year to the next as they were being targeted in an aggressive takeover.

The key mindset to maintain is that you should be ready to scale down the business rapidly. It's easy to hire when growth necessitates, but be prepared to lose staff for a rapid scale down if needed. This does not mean having a yo-yo hiring approach but having a strategy of scaling ready to deploy when required.

The criteria or triggers for scaling down should be agreed upon within the shareholder team (if there are multiple shareholders) ahead of time, allowing quick, decisive action with minimal conflict. The triggers for this action should be well defined and could be things like profitability over a period, cash flow metrics, or measures of team morale.

Understand that it should never be easy to let people go. We are, after all, in a people business, and therefore, care and compassion are critical. However, also recognize that by letting certain people go, you are protecting those who remain.

Save for a Rainy Day

This principle does not just apply to your personal life. In business, too, it's imperative that finances are set aside in good times to cover for potential downturns. As a leadership team, set a target for what kind of cash balance should always be maintained within the business ahead of other expenditures. This might be, for example, four months' wages and salaries that are not to be touched other than to meet these bills should there be a cash shortfall.

It's also prudent to set up lines of credit or debtor finance with the banks when business is going well, even if these are never used. They can come in very handy in a downturn. The other strategy we employed at Bluleader was to have clear agreement from shareholders that cash injections might be needed and that all shareholders would be able to contribute in proportion to their shareholding if called upon.

The Risk Register

Many consider a risk register to be more applicable to a project being delivered. It is, however, just as relevant for your business. On an annual basis, draw up a new risk register that is a living document. (Update it constantly as new risks arise.) It should identify the risks that could affect your business, how likely the risks are, and their possible consequences.

Once possible risks have been identified, create a risk-treatment plan to prioritize them, and write down actions that can be taken to prevent the issue or at least lessen its impact. The risk register is a great tool that allows you as owners to identify worst-case scenarios before they occur and to have preprepared approaches that have already been agreed upon should the scenarios occur. This minimizes potential conflict and allows for decisive action when required.

Key Takeaways

1. Improve on the worst-case scenario to reduce stress levels.

2. Use day-tight compartments to focus only on today's tasks and avoid carrying over worries to the next day.

3. Adopt the role of a problem-solver or escalation point, similar to a doctor, as the business grows.

4. Be ready to scale down if external forces affect the business.

CONCLUSION

Well, we've made it through this exploration, and now your journey begins. This book started out with the tale of a business owner who is overworked, tired, never takes vacations, barely spends time with his family, and is ready to give up. I hope that after you've read the book in its entirety that you're no longer thinking about being that business owner but one who has a prosperous business, a fat bank account, plenty of time for family, vacations, and hobbies and is ready to grow and scale his business into one that gives him that very life.

I began by telling my story because it's the stories of those who have been there before that help shape our vision for a better future. Next, I talked about the benefits of growing your business rather than staying complacent in where you are right now.

Then, we shifted into mindset. Without the proper mindset to keep yourself in check, it's very easy to fall back into old habits or become discouraged and disgruntled. Once you got your mindset in check, I asked you to envision your Big Hairy Audacious Goal and where you want to be in three to five years. From there, we worked backward to assess where you are right now, your Active State, and how to bridge the gap from today to a better future.

Finally, we talked about filling out your A3 Strategy and how to set yourself up for success with your execution plans. By now, you are fully equipped to take action and work toward your exit strategy.

Reaching the Peak

By and large, your BHAG is what keeps you and your ownership group aligned. Everything we've discussed in this book up until this point is all about you reaching your peak. For some, the peak could very well be your exit strategy, as discussed in chapter 4. Another option could be one owner selling off his shares to the rest of the group.

Drawing a parallel with athletics, when you're an Olympian, the peak is winning a gold medal. But once you've won it, you'll think to yourself, "Okay, what's next?" It's essential to have that "what's next" goal identified both personally and in your business.

When Millionaire Mentor asked this very question to us at Bluleader, our initial response was, "What do you mean? To keep making more money every year!" What he made us realize was that, with that approach, we weren't truly aiming for anything at all.

In another instance, I've been working with a client who, when I asked him this same question, said he'd like to do $9 million in revenue in five years' time. That's great, but why? What's the purpose? He didn't know. A number on its own is simply not good enough. Instead, do you want to retire? Spend more time with your family? There has to be a destination and a why.

If reaching the top of Mount Everest is your peak, that is fine, but what is your why? More than likely, it's the bragging rights to say you've done it or, even better, to catch that incredible view from the top!

All in all, if exiting is the goal, the sum of money you want to walk away with shouldn't be the money you want to spend for the rest of your life. It should be your capital. You may want to invest in properties with the proceeds, take care of yourself and your family, or donate to charity. Now you have a comfortable retirement, and those funds won't keep shrinking.

When working with clients, once we've identified the peak and their why, I start to see faces light up with joy and hope. It must be something that really excites you, because you'll do crazy things to get there. If you don't have that why identified, you will end up doing things halfheartedly and will likely not reach your goal.

From Sweat to Scale: Get Out There and Grow!

I'll close this book by giving you an ordered list of action steps. Some of these are simple, while others will take time and effort. However, if you've read the book cover to cover, you have all the tools you need.

1. **Get your mindset right.** Understand why it's important to grow. Get yourself off the tools, and start running your business like an army general rather than a team captain. Identify the smartest people in your company, and give

them measurable responsibilities and clear expectations. Build a culture to keep your top performers.

2. **Identify your ideal company.** Think long and hard about your BHAG, agree upon it with your shareholders, and stick to it. Then, identify your value proposition, core competencies, and the market in which you'll operate. Set goals for three to five years and then for one year.

3. **Assess your Active State.** Take our online assessment to see where your business is today. Engage with your employees, fellow shareholders, and your customers to get a realistic point of view of your business's current value proposition, core competencies, and market.

4. **Pinpoint the delta.** How far are you from your Target State as it stands today? Assess how efficient your eight "always-on" engines are in the present moment.

5. **Fill out the A3 Strategy.** Use the steps in chapter 16 to completely fill out the A3 Strategy, and distribute it among your shareholders and employees. This should be prominently displayed in your physical office space if you have one.

6. **Set up the scaffolding and drill down.** Work to improve your existing engines and build any that do not yet exist. Determine your budget and hiring needs. Take your 1-year goals and break them down quarter by quarter month by month, and week by week. Ensure employees know their roles and responsibilities, and hold them accountable to them.

7. **Put accountability measures in place.** Be sure to have

weekly meetings with each manager to keep them on track with their KPIs. If you have fellow shareholders, put measures in place to hold one another accountable. Do whatever you can to enlist outside help (consultants) to hold you accountable as well.

8. **Wash, rinse, and repeat.** Check in on yourself. Are you sticking to the plan? If you are straying in any of the above areas, take steps to get yourself back on track.

I sincerely hope that my experiences in growing and scaling my business toward my lucrative, life-changing exit (and helping others to do the same) has not only inspired you to follow suit but also helped you understand the exact steps you need to take to live the life you've always desired.

This book was the culmination of my sweating and my scaling to better help those who come after me to achieve amazing business and personal results. It was a labor of love and passion. It was my story. Now it's time for you to get out there and write yours.

That's it. Now, wipe the sweat off your brow, and get out there and grow! It's time to scale up in ways you never have and realize your ultimate dreams!

ACKNOWLEDGMENTS

To be honest, I never thought I would want or would think to write a book like this. However, due to the encouragement to do so and the support of those around me, I have endeavored to capture on paper my experience of building a tech services business over the years. I really want this to be a collection of all I have learned that will positively impact business owners and help them avoid some of the many mistakes (which became learnings) that I made. The takeaway being that, despite all the setbacks, I did break through and achieve my dream outcome. Through the ups and downs, I had an amazing support team whom I would like to acknowledge and thank:

Firstly, my ever-supportive wife, Eleanor. She has walked this whole journey with me, right from the start. As a matter fact, she was the one who "pushed" me to go out on my own and start Bluleader. She was my greatest supporter when I started the business all the way through to this point. Her support was both emotional and practical. I know that my success would never have happened if I did not have her by my side.

My three sons, Daniel, Michael, and Matthew, who have had to listen to "business speak" for years and now have grown into motivated young men who push me constantly. They have always been understanding of the sacrifices we made early on and have had the best attitudes through it all.

The Bluleader team that we built and that was my home. There would be no story without them.

I would also like to acknowledge all the other scaffolding support that has been a part of my mastermind over the years and has helped me get to the point of this book, specifically:

- Tony Hughes, sales guru and friend

- Dr. Ian Rutherford, my friend and "psychology advisor," who helped me apply some powerful principles I would never have thought of myself

- Hernus Carelsen, who was my "always-on" advisor throughout the Bluleader growth journey

- Robin Apfel, my business partner at Bluleader; without him, we'd never have achieved the scale that we did

- Romano Formaggio, my brother who, through his own business success, has been an inspiration, thanks to his constant display of integrity and business savvy. He has always been a willing advisor and a great supporter to me.

ABOUT THE AUTHOR

Marco Formaggio is a seasoned entrepreneur and technology expert with more than two decades of experience in the industry. He started his career as a mechanical engineer in the early 1990s and later moved into engineering sales and technology services consulting.

Marco quickly rose to prominence as a high-performing SAP sales and distribution specialist and was an early expert in CRM implementation when the technology rose to prominence in the early 2000s. In 2007, he founded Bluleader, a niche SAP customer experience partner, which quickly grew to become the leading partner in the Australian market and was eventually acquired by global NYSE-listed company DXC Technology.

After completing his earnout at DXC, Marco founded Sweat2Scale. The business aims to help growing technology services businesses scale successfully and sustainably by sharing hands-on learnings and applying a structured framework to growth.

Marco resides in Sydney, Australia, with his wife and three sons, and is passionate about helping others grow successful businesses while maintaining a healthy work-life balance.

Check out sweat2scale.com for more of Marco's thoughts on growing and scaling technology services businesses and to find out more about his one-on-one coaching services for your business.

LinkedIn: https://www.linkedin.com/company/sweat2scale/

RECOMMENDED READING

Much of what I have learned is from trial and error, real-life experience, and a handful of highly impactful books that I have listed below. I strongly suggest you read them too.

Good to Great: Why Some Companies Make the Leap and Others Don't, Jim Collins

This book reinforces the reasons that great companies exist. Some may think this book is only for big companies since Collins profiles some marquee names, but there are many powerful principles that can be applied to businesses of any size.

Mastering the Rockefeller Habits: What You Must Do to Increase the Value of Your Growing Firm, Verne Harnish

This is a must-read for any fast-growing business!

The Breakthrough Company: How Everyday Companies Become Extraordinary Performers, Keith McFarland

This detailed book delves into how companies can break through from average to great.

Influence: The Psychology of Persuasion, Robert Cialdini

The persuasion triggers within are so powerful and effective that every business owner should understand how to apply these principles.

How to Stop Worrying and Start Living: Time-TestedMethods for Conquering Worry, Dale Carnegie

I was especially impacted by the concept of day-tight compartments and, when facing a crisis, to:

Step 1: Analyze that situation to determine the worst-possible scenario if you fail.

Step 2: Ask yourself if you could live with the worst-possible scenario if it were to happen.

Step 3: Focus on doing everything you can to improve the situation, so you end up with a better outcome than the worst-case scenario.

Who: The A Method for Hiring, Geoff Smart and Randy Street

This must-read provides a concrete method for hiring people.

The Five Dysfunctions of a Team: A Leadership Fable, Patrick Lencioni

This was a massively impactful book for me in terms of team dynamics and my role as a leader.

Death by Meeting: A Leadership Fable About Solving the Most Painful Problem in Business, Patrick Lencioni

Two books by Lencioni, I know! This book was a game changer for me in understanding the criticality of meeting rhythm—something that did not come naturally for me.

Rich Dad's Cashflow Quadrant: Rich Dad's Guide to Financial Freedom, Robert Kiyosaki

I realize this one seems a bit out of left field in this list, but in terms of mindset, it's spot on. You need to see that you are creating a business, not a job where you simply employ yourself.

The 7 Habits of Highly Effective People, Stephen Covey

It's a classic. It highlights so many of the mindset principles required for business owners and high performers.

Managing the Professional Service Firm, David H. Maister

This is a seminal book for the professional services firm owner.

The Joshua Principle, Tony J. Hughes

Hughes presents a super practical approach to sales in a novel format. Also, I suggest you read his other two sales books, *Combo Prospecting* and *Tech-Powered Sales*. Hughes is a world leader in B2B sales and has worked for years in the tech world.

I will periodically add to my list of recommended reading on my website, sweat2scale.com. Please check regularly and follow us on LinkedIn for more insightful posts: https://www.linkedin.com/company/sweat2scale/.

NOTES

1   Collins, Jim. *Good to Great: Why Some Companies Make the Leap and Others Don't.* New York: HarperCollins, 2001. 41.

2   Flatow, Ira. *Present at the Future: From Evolution to Nanotechnology, Candid and Controversial Conversations on Science and Nature.* New York: HarperCollins, 2007. 263–4.

3   Gilligan, Walter. "M&A Trends in the Global Professional Services Industry." Global PMI Partners. April 16, 2023. https://gpmip .com/ma-trends-in-the-global-professional-services-industry/.

4   "Office of Digital Services Industries (ODSI)." International Trade Administration. U.S. Department of Commerce. Accessed March 14, 2023. https://www.trade.gov/about-us/office-digital-services -industries.

5   "Industry Outlook." FirstHand. Accessed March 14, 2023. https:// firsthand.co/industries/information-technology-consulting /industry-outlook.

6   Christian, Bruce. "Analysys Mason Predicts SMB IT Spending Will Increase This Year." *ChannelVision Magazine.* Beka Business Media. August 22, 2022. https://channelvisionmag.com/ analysys-mason-predicts-smb-it-spending-will-increase-this-year/.

7   Mearian, Lucas. "Talent War to Push CIOs Toward Consultancies, Managed Services in '22." *Computerworld.* IDG Communications,

Inc. January 20, 2022. https://www.computerworld.com
/article/3647749/talent-war-to-push-cios-toward-consultancies
-managed-services-in-22.html.

8   Armeson, Spencer and Jeff Thompson. "How to budget for
    enterprise software." *Strategic Finance*. The Free Library by Farlex.
    January 1, 2005. https://www.thefreelibrary.com/How+to
    +budget+for+enterprise+software-a0127980927.

9   Robbins, Tony. "Grow your business with an exit
    strategy." October 11, 2017. YouTube video, 0:51.https://
    www.youtube.com/watch?v=K4CaG_lRK18.

10 Mattke, Dr. Angela C. "How Much Should I Expect My Baby to
    Grow in the First Year?" Mayo Clinic. January 11, 2023. https://
    www.mayoclinic.org/healthy-lifestyle/infant-and-toddler-health
    /expert-answers/infant-growth/faq-20058037.

11 "Amazon's Two-Pizza Rule: One Simple Rule for Maximizing
    Meeting Effectiveness." Directorpoint. February 11, 2021. https://
    landing.directorpoint.com/blog/amazon-two-pizza-rule/.

12 McCarthy, Niall. "The Share of Americans Holding a Passport Has
    Increased Dramatically in Recent Years [Infographic]." *Forbes*. Forbes
    Media LLC. January 11, 2018. https://www.forbes.com/sites
    /niallmccarthy/2018/01/11/the-share-of-americans-holding-a
    -passport-has-increased-dramatically-in-recent-years
    -infographic/?sh=2d9c186e3c16.

13 Bromberg-Martin, Ethan S., Masayuki Matsumoto, and Okihide
    Hikosaka. "Dopamine in Motivational Control: Rewarding,
    Aversive, and Alerting." *Neuron* 68, no. 5 (2010): 815–834.
    https://www.cell.com/neuron/fulltext/S0896-6273(10)00938-4.

14 Hill, Napoleon. *The Law of Success in Sixteen
    Lessons*. New York: Tribeca Books, 1928.

15 Sharma, Robin S. "Never be a prisoner of your past. Become the
    architect of your future." Quotepark, n.d. https://quotepark.com
    /quotes/1117662-robin-s-sharma-never-be-a-prisoner-of-your
    -past-become-the-archi/.

16 "Should You Hire People That Are Smarter Than You? A Data-
    Driven Answer." Leveling Up. https://www.levelingup.com/hiring
    /should-you-hire-people-that-are-smarter-than-you-a-data-driven
    -answer.

17 Ilgaz, Zeynep. "Why You Should Hire People Who Are Smarter Than You." LinkedIn. February 19, 2015. https://www.linkedin.com/pulse/why-you-should-hire-people-who-smarter-than-zeynep-ilgaz/.

18 Jobs, Steve. "Focusing is about saying no – Steve Jobs (WWDC '97)." uploaded by Erin 'Folletto' Casali. June 26, 2011. YouTube video, 3:05. https://www.youtube.com/watch?v=H8eP99neOVs.

19 "2021 Professional Services Maturity™ Benchmark." Service Performance Insight, LLC. February 2021. 36. https://globalwhitepaper.com/wp-content/uploads/2021/04/92830_2021PSMB_Unit4.pdf.

20 Collins, Jim. *Good to Great: Why Some Companies Make the Leap and Others Don't.* New York: HarperCollins, 2001. 90.

21 Long, Adam. "Why Steve Jobs Killed 70% of Apple's Products: A Lesson on Range Architecture." Hello Step Change. February 1, 2016. https://blog.hellostepchange.com/blog/why-steve-jobs-killed-70-of-apples-products-a-lesson-on-range-architecture.

22 "How this firm achieved 60% growth by going niche." Sweat2Scale. March 8, 2023. https://www.sweat2scale.com/video/how-this-firm-achieved-60-growth-by-going-niche.

23 U2. "11 O'Clock Tick Tock." Island Records. 1980.

24 Clark, Tim. "No More Brilliant Jerks: Arianna Huffington on the Power of Changing Corporate Culture." *Forbes*. December 3, 2018. https://www.forbes.com/sites/sap/2018/12/03/no-more-brilliant-jerks-arianna-huffington-on-the-power-of-changing-corporate-culture.

25 "Travis Kalanick Resigns as Uber C.E.O." *New York Times*. June 21, 2017. https://www.nytimes.com/2017/06/21/technology/uber-ceo-travis-kalanick.html.

26 Haselton, Todd. "Uber's CEO is out: Here's everything that went wrong with Uber this year." CNBC. June 21, 2017. https://www.cnbc.com/2017/06/21/uber-timeline-why-did-ceo-travis-kalanick-leave.html.

27 Bishop, Todd. "Exclusive: Satya Nadella reveals Microsoft's new mission statement, sees 'tough choices' ahead." June 25, 2015. https://www.geekwire.com/2015/exclusive-satya-nadella-reveals-microsofts-new-mission-statement-sees-more-tough-choices-ahead/.

28 "James Stockdale." Wikipedia. https://
en.wikipedia.org/wiki/James_Stockdale.

29 Collins, Jim. "Stockdale Paradox: A Message for
Uncertain Times." Uploaded by Jim Collins - Good to
Great. March 31, 2020. YouTube video, 6:41. https://
www.youtube.com/watch?v=GvWWO7F9kQY.

30 Lencioni, Patrick M. "Make Your Values Mean Something." *Harvard
Business Review*. July 2002. https://hbr.org/2002/07/make-your
-values-mean-something.

31 PrinciplesYou. "PrinciplesYou from Ray Dalio."
2023. https://principlesyou.com/.

32 Cutter, Chip. "An employee slammed hedge fund giant Ray Dalio in
an email. Dalio loved it so much, he talked about it in a TED Talk."
LinkedIn. April 16, 2017. https://www.linkedin.com/pulse
/employee-sent-hedge-fund-giant-ray-dalio-critical-email-chip
-cutter/.

33 "How to Create Your BHAG—Big Hairy Audacious Goal."
Rhythm Systems. 2021. https://www.rhythmsystems.com/bhag-big
-hairy-audacious-goal.

34 Collins, Jim. "BHAG." Jim Collins. https://www.jimcollins.com
/concepts/bhag.html.

35 "BHAG: Why the Most Successful Companies Set Ambitious,
Long-Term Goals & Why Yours Should Too." Growth Institute.
May 10, 2019. https://blog.growthinstitute.com/scale
-up-blueprint/bhag-big-hairy-audacious-goal.

36 Hill, Napoleon. Exact source unknown.

37 Stalk, George Jr., and Thomas M. Hout. "Erecting Scaffolding." In
The Breakthrough Company, New York: Harper Business, 2008.

38 Elsey, Emma-Louise. "Coaching Tools 101: The Urgent-Important
Matrix—What and How to Use It!" The Coaching Tools Company.
September 22, 2022. https://www.thecoachingtoolscompany.com
/coaching-tools-101-what-is-the-urgent-important-matrix/.

39 Lencioni, Patrick. "The Fable." In*Death by Meeting*. New Jersey:
Jossey-Bass, 2004.

40 Collins, Jim. *Good to Great*. 104–8.

41 Spencer, Leon. "Deloitte Acquires Presence of IT in Landmark
Deal." ARN. IDG Communications. October 23, 2019.

https://www.arnnet.com.au/article/667800/deloitte-acquires
-presence-it-landmark-deal/.

42 Carelsen, Hernus. "Can I be empathetic and demand high
performance?" Sweat2Scale. https://www.sweat2scale.com
/video/empathy-and-high-performance.

43 Hoffman, Reid, Ben Casnocha, and Chris Yeh. "Your Company
Is Not a Family." *Harvard Business Review*. June 17, 2014.
https://hbr.org/2014/06/your-company-is-not-a-family.

44 Carnegie, Dale. *How to Stop Worrying and Start Living*.
London: Simon & Schuster, 1948.

45 Carnegie, How to Stop Worrying and Start Living.

Together, Let's Take Action Now

and Follow the High Road to Breakthrough

Follow me on Linkedin to receive my up to date, relevant content for tech services business owners:
www.linkedin.com/in/marcoformaggio/

Unlock your business's true potential today! Claim your FREE consultation to uncover the root causes holding back your growth and discover your roadmap to success.
www.sweat2scale.com/#Contact

If you enjoyed
ELEVATE YOUR ENTERPRISE,
please leave a review
on Goodreads
or on the retailer site
where you purchased
this book.